T0168105

Wing Chun Warrior

"The story of Duncan Leung — childhood friend of Bruce Lee and disciple of *Wing Chun* master Yip Man — is valuable not only for the insights it offers into Chinese martial arts but also for its portrayal of the lost Hong Kong of the 1950s and 1960s. Reading Ken Ing's *Wing Chun Warrior*, which chronicles Leung's *kung fu* escapades, will be a jarring revelation to anyone familiar with the manic but orderly and largely peaceful city of seven million people that is Hong Kong today. The city described by Ing is a place where *kung fu* practitioners wielded eight-chop knives in the streets and literally battled their way from one martial arts studio to another to prove their fighting prowess." — *Asia Times*

"Wonderfully informal and instructive... There are many stories and personal revelations that should be fascinating, intriguing and occasionally infuriating to students of this style and those interested in the clouds surrounding the Hong Kong days of Bruce Lee and others." — Ted Mancuso, martial arts instructor and writer

"A great addition to your collection." — *Wing Chun Archive*

Wing Chun Warrior

*The True Tales of Wing Chun
Kung Fu Master Duncan Leung,
Bruce Lee's Fighting Companion*

Ken Ing, M.D.

BLACKSMITH BOOKS

WING CHUN WARRIOR

ISBN 978-988-17742-2-4

Published by Blacksmith Books
Unit 26, 19/F, Block B, Wah Lok Industrial Centre,
37-41 Shan Mei Street, Fo Tan, Hong Kong
Tel: (+852) 2877 7899
www.blacksmithbooks.com

© 2010 Ken Ing

Third printing 2018

The author asserts the moral right to
be identified as the author of this work.

Edited by Richard S. Marten
Illustrations by Siu Hoi-on

Dedicated to the memory of Duncan's *Sifu* (師父)

Yip Man (葉問)
1893-1972

Yip Man introduced *Wing Chun Kung Fu* to Hong Kong in 1949, and was the paramount leader of the sixth generation teaching there. He taught Duncan Leung wholeheartedly and unreservedly. Between 1955 and 1959, he privately instructed Duncan in the practical application of *Wing Chun Kung Fu*. Yip Man passed away on December 1, 1972.

And dedicated also to the memory of

Bruce Lee (李小龍)
1940-1973

Bruce Lee, the *Wing Chun Kung Fu* legend, was Duncan Leung's childhood friend. He introduced Duncan to *Sifu* Yip Man and *Wing Chun Kung Fu*, and practiced with him between 1955 and 1958. Even long after his passing, Bruce Lee is still the most famous martial artist in the world. Through Bruce Lee's films, *Wing Chun Kung Fu* became one of the most popular and practiced martial arts. His untimely death on July 20, 1973 left a void that has never been filled.

Application is the only way to verify the truth
實 踐 是 抵 達 真 理 的 唯 一 途 徑
(*shi jian shi di da zhen li di wei yi yu jing*)
Buddha, c. 500 B.C.

"I am somebody who is nobody, and I have spent a lifetime dreaming, learning and practicing fighting. I have had many chances to see if what I know works. The material I have presented in this book may not mean much to you, but I put my life in danger for the knowledge. I have fought for real and, having tried these techniques, I have refined them to eliminate error. I am still alive because of them. These techniques worked for me and they should work for you."

From the 'Forward' to *The Law Enforcement Manual of Martial Arts Self-Defense,* Duncan Leung Shiu-hung (梁紹鴻), 1978.

Contents

PREFACE

This book is about the adventure of a living *Wing Chun Kung Fu* master. Details of his unique relationships with two of the most famous martial artists of the 20th century – Yip Man and screen star Bruce Lee – are revealed for the first time.

It is also the first time that true fighting episodes of all these three masters have been revealed in print.

Duncan Leung is not only a great pugilist; he is also an articulate exponent of martial arts. A natural prodigy born with the inherent talent to become a good fighter, fortune blessed him with the rare opportunity to learn from and practice with Yip Man, the revered *Wing Chun* master, who graciously accepted him as his private student and formal disciple.

Yip Man recognized talent when he saw it. He taught Duncan Leung privately, wholeheartedly and unreservedly how to apply all the *Wing Chun Kung Fu* he knew and instilled in him the martial virtues expected of a great fighter.

Fortune also blessed Duncan Leung with plentiful opportunities to apply his knowledge. He was born in an era when fighting in the streets and *Kung Fu* studios of Hong Kong was dealt with more leniently by the law. As a result, he was able to amass fighting experience that was to prove invaluable.

Between 1955 and 1959, he defeated many well-known masters of established Chinese *Kung Fu* systems at their studios. When he lost, his *Sifu* would point out to him the intricacies of each system and teach him how to counter them. Duncan never lost a rematch. His breadth of fighting experience against different *Kung Fu* systems is second to none.

When he furthered his education in Australia between 1959 and 1963, he was surprised to discover that Western boxing experts were the most difficult opponents to deal with, and boxing techniques were *Wing Chun*'s natural antagonists. However, he had the techniques and ability to counter them.

In 1964, Duncan rescued an old man from a beating outside a theatre in Hong Kong. In gratitude, the old man offered to teach him the secrets of close fighting, which included the art of knife fighting and silencing an opponent barehanded. These lethal close range techniques gave him the confidence needed to finish off an opponent if necessary. Duncan would later teach these to elite military units.

When he opened his first *Wing Chun* studio in New York City in 1974, he was challenged practically every day by martial arts practitioners of every school, such as *Tae Kwon Do*, *Karate*, Thai boxing, *Wing Chun* and other *Kung Fu* systems. Ultimately, to save time, he went to visit every studio and offered himself up for challenge. He was undefeated, and his vast fighting experience against different martial arts systems was put beyond question.

Since moving to Virginia Beach in 1976, he has taught U.S. Navy SEAL Teams Two and Four, members of the FBI, local SWAT teams, and other law enforcement agencies throughout the world.

Bruce Lee modified the *Wing Chun Kung Fu* he learned from Yip Man and incorporated other forms of martial arts to found *Jeet Kune Do* (截拳道). Yet, since Lee's death, it is *Wing Chun Kung Fu*, rather than *Jeet Kune Do,* which has become one of the most popular and, paradoxically, abused *Kung Fu* systems in the world.

Duncan Leung has applied the *Wing Chun Kung Fu* he learned

from Yip Man through voluminous fighting experience. Today, almost half a century after meeting Yip Man, Duncan teaches *Applied Wing Chun,* consistently proving to his students that this system can be used successfully in combat without incorporating other forms of martial arts. His mission is to pass on *Applied Wing Chun* as he learned it. Most recently he has trained a select group of Chinese teenagers to be world-class fighters capable of winning Free Fight competitions and tournaments. His purpose in doing so is to demonstrate that *Wing Chun Kung Fu* is an effective martial art, and not a mere performing art.

The events depicted herein are true. The author has concentrated on those that are both interesting and which highlight an ethical issue. Although his inherent modesty did not facilitate my task, I have confirmed with *Sifu* Leung the episodes related in these pages. I elicited much information about *Wing Chun* by posing simple, even naïve questions, so that novices like myself and the uninformed reader can better understand certain fundamental concepts, as well as the logic, philosophy and science behind the art.

As a matter of respect to deceased and living martial artists, the author has not been permitted to identify certain individuals and martial arts styles in the telling of specific events. The author – and no doubt many curious readers – can only hope that Duncan may one day change his mind in this respect. Certainly, a comprehensive analysis of the various martial art forms would be of tremendous value to aspiring martial artists who wish to know the pros and cons of each style in combat. However, for the moment, we must be content with the information that the Warrior has made available. During the writing of this chronicle, the author has discovered that Duncan Leung is an unusual and distinct personality; his disposition is uniquely his own.

While possessed of a fine sense of humor – even fond of practical jokes – Duncan is very serious about *Wing Chun* and never makes light of it. He goes out of his way to defend *Wing Chun* whenever and wherever it is called into question. In relating his fighting episodes – whether he won or lost – Duncan's emphasis is on accuracy; he meticulously avoids exaggeration. About his commercial and financial interests, he is much less serious, and in speaking about his school years, even after decades, he cannot hide his delight in his often mischievous adventures. Unfortunately the author is not permitted to publish many of these at this time. Perhaps one day, if he decides to write his autobiography, Duncan will recount them, revealing the playful side of his personality. Yet, it should be said that any would-be opponents who might think that Duncan is strictly physical should have second thoughts: beware of his traps and perfect timing.

Destiny

As is true of human relations, literary conception is often unintentional rather than premeditated. Such was the case with *Wing Chun Warrior*. If one places credence in fate, predestination, or karma, this work will not dissuade you from such belief; there are several incidents in *Wing Chun Warrior* which might be accounted for by these doctrines. *Yuan* (緣) or *Yuanfen* (緣分) is a Buddhist term used to describe a predestined relationship, one which is not explained by logic or more mundane factors.

I was introduced to Duncan Leung in June 1999, at a meeting in Panyu (番禺), then an independent city southwest of Guangzhou (廣州), the capital of Guangdong (廣東) Province, China. Over the next two years, we encountered each other casually on a number of occasions. As far as I knew at the time, Duncan was an international businessman commuting between China and the United States. More than that, I did not know.

In June 2001, at a breakfast gathering, again in Panyu (which in the intervening time had become a district of Guangzhou), a certain Mr Poon, a close friend of Duncan, asked me a casual question: "Do you know what Duncan's dream is? He wants to open a *Wing Chun* academy and, hopefully, discover a few talented students so that he can teach them all the *Wing Chun Kung Fu* he knows."

"What?" I replied in amazement, "He knows *Wing Chun*?"

When I asked Duncan about this, he said that *Wing Chun* was his life. Challenging him, I said: "Everybody knows Bruce Lee and his *Sifu*, Yip Man. But I have never heard of you."

To my astonishment, Duncan responded, "My *Sifu* was Yip Man. I was his private student and formal disciple."

"So, there are others who also learned from Yip Man. How do I know your *Wing Chun* is better than theirs? How many *Wing Chun* instructors are there? If my kids want to learn tennis, I would send them to the Bollettieri Tennis Academy. They have produced kids who became world champions."

"What *Sifu* taught me was how to apply *Wing Chun Kung Fu*. In those days, we learned and practiced through fighting. We picked fights all the time. Hundreds of fights, street fights, fights in rival studios."

"You must be kidding. Hundreds of fights?"

"Yes, hundreds."

I was more interested in his fights than in his *Wing Chun* Academy. I tried to convince him that he should learn the Bollettieri way.

"Perhaps you should try to discover a few talented boys first. Teach them and prepare them for tournaments, for free if necessary."

"Free of charge?"

"Yes, free of charge. Your priority is to produce champions to prove that your *Applied Wing Chun* is effective against other martial arts and other *Wing Chun* systems."

"How?"

"To attract potential talents, you should try to establish your name first. Writing your true fighting stories, for example, would probably be an effective way to make yourself known. Let the stories speak for themselves."

"Ken, forget it. I am too busy with my business. I don't have the time or interest to write."

"Look, I am retired and I have plenty of time. Tell me your stories. Let me record and write them down for you. People love real things."

"I wouldn't mind."

The more I listened, the more I became fascinated – not only by Duncan's stories, but also by the techniques, logic, philosophy, art and science of *Applied Wing Chun*, which represented a revolution in *Kung Fu* and martial arts.

Having spoken to dozens of his colleagues, disciples, students, friends and family members, and police and military he has trained – and as I contemplate what he has endured during the course of his *Kung Fu* career – it is difficult to believe that this living embodiment of the martial arts has survived and now lives on in the 21st century.

Now approaching the age of 60 myself, I am studying *Applied Wing Chun*, a martial arts system founded by a woman to give smaller and weaker individuals an edge against those who are larger and more powerful. *Applied Wing Chun* is fun and safe. It offers the opportunity to learn self-confidence, self-defense, self-esteem and discipline, both physically and mentally. I would not hesitate to recommend it to anyone. Just ask your instructor one simple question: "Did you learn and practice *Wing Chun* or *Kung Fu* through fighting, and how often did you fight?" You will be surprised to hear that many *Wing Chun* or *Kung Fu* instructors can teach you how to perform, and yet they cannot teach you how to protect yourself because they themselves do not have the practical knowledge.

ACKNOWLEDGEMENTS

This book could not have been written without the blessing and cooperation of the Warrior himself. Why he has decided to permit the release of these stories now and not earlier – and through a novice writer – is perhaps a function of *yuan* (緣). My personal belief is that I am but one of a number of individuals who are destined to assist in the mission of passing on *Applied Wing Chun* to future generations. I am honored and forever grateful for the opportunity to share some of Duncan Leung's unique history with the interested reader.

I am privileged to have Mr Richard S. Marten as my editor. Mr Marten, an attorney by training, is a writer, film producer, businessman and friend of Duncan Leung. I am deeply grateful to him for undertaking this unenviable responsibility, and for his kindness in devoting a great deal of time to help me complete this volume for publication. His precise, concise and fluent edition has not only made reading *Wing Chun Warrior* much more enjoyable but also made writing the Chinese version a much simpler task.

Special thanks go to Professor Li Hon-ki for permission to publish his intriguing testimonial. He is unashamed in recounting his personal experience which, he hopes, will serve as a reminder to aspirants of the pitfalls of learning *Kung Fu,* or any martial art for that matter, unless one has the fortune (or *yuan*) to encounter a true master with real knowledge and experience.

Dr John Newton is a close friend and probably the most faithful fan and follower of the Warrior. He is knowledgeable about Duncan

Leung, *Wing Chun Kung Fu* in general and *Applied Wing Chun* in particular. I am indebted to him not only for his generosity in sharing this knowledge with me, but also for his time and effort in correcting the numerous mistakes in the manuscript of this book.

I wish to thank Dr Jarley Koo, my good friend since high school, for reading the manuscript, rendering honest comments, and offering valuable suggestions.

Mr Siu Hoi-on, veteran comic book artist who specializes in drawing fighting scenes, asserts that comic book fighting scenes are invariably fantastical. The artists draw strictly from their imaginations, presenting the same to the unwary reader who is none the wiser. This is the first time in his career that he has illustrated actual fighting scenes. I truly appreciate his patience, professionalism and attention to detail in bringing real events to life on the printed page.

I must also thank Mr Gary Liu for kindly assisting in what, for me, was the formidable challenge of making the best use of the computer.

Last but not least, I am grateful to Ms Li Mei-ron whose patience in listening to the episodes and efficiently typing them in Chinese helped translate my thoughts into proper words.

As the writer Stephen King has commented: *Writing is about enriching the lives of those who will read your work, and enriching your own life, as well. It's about getting up, getting well, and getting over.* Thus should my own motivation be clear.

NOTE TO THE READER

Wing Chun, short for *Wing Chun Kung Fu*, is a system of martial art. The term 'martial art' encompasses every form of fighting system in the world, such as *Karate, Kung Fu, Judo, Ju-Jitsu, Tae Kwon Do*, Thai Boxing, Western Boxing, etc.

In China, fighting systems are generally called *Wuye* (武藝), *Wushu* (武術), *Guoshu* (國術), *Wugong* (武功), or *Gongfu* (功夫) in Putonghua and *Kung Fu* (功夫) in Cantonese. The Chinese character 武 (*Wu*) implies 'fighting' and the character 藝 (*Ye*) signifies 'art'. The most appropriate term for martial arts in the Chinese language is thus *Wuye* (武藝), yet it is seldom used.

Kung Fu was the term originally used by Bruce Lee in his interviews, demonstrations, movies and books during the 1960s and 1970s. Bruce Lee was born in the United States, but raised and educated in Hong Kong. Cantonese was his mother tongue, and therefore the term *Kung Fu* was his natural choice. It remains the most popular term employed in the West and outside Mainland China.

The term *Kung Fu* also happens to refer to the levels of attainment in various skilled trades, such as cookery, carpentry and masonry. Rather than asking, "How good are you?" meaning "How good is your skill?" one might enquire: "How good is your *kung fu*?"

Canton is the Western name for the city of Guangzhou (廣州), the capital of Guangdong Province (廣東省). Cantonese is the Western term for the dialect spoken by the residents of Canton and its vicinities. The dialect is now called Guangdonghua

(廣東話) or Yueyu (粵語), even though not all the residents of Guangdong Province can converse in it. It is widely spoken in the Pearl River Delta, which includes Hong Kong (a former British colony), Macau (a former Portuguese colony), Shenzhen (深圳), Guangzhou, Foshan (佛山) and Shunde (順德). Cantonese is also spoken in parts of Guangxi Province (廣西省) – Nanning (南寧), the provincial capital, for example – and in overseas Chinese communities. An estimated 200 million people around the globe speak this language.

Mandarin – variously called Putonghua (普通話) or Guo Yu (國語) in Chinese – is the language that was historically spoken in Northern China in and around Beijing (北京), the capital. Putonghua is a newer term for Guo Yu introduced since the birth of the People's Republic of China in 1949. Putonghua is the official language of China and its 1.3 billion citizens. However, Guo Yu is still the term preferred in many areas such as Taiwan and overseas Chinese communities.

In this book, Chinese characters are transliterated from Putonghua, the official standard Chinese pronunciation, and bracketed in *hanyu pinyin* (漢語拼音). Chinese characters in classical forms are bracketed for those who are unfamiliar with Putonghua and simplified forms. However, pronunciation and spelling of familiar terms, proper names, and places have been left unchanged.

Spelling and Transliteration

Much time and effort has been expended in the dispute over the exact spelling of the Chinese characters 詠春. Just as pronunciation differs from dialect to dialect, so does transliteration into European languages. It is sufficient for readers to recognize the

Chinese characters. No superiority, purity, authenticity or mystery is indicated by variant transliteration, whether it be *Wing Chun*, *Wing Tsun* or *Ving Chun*, etc.

The Chinese character 咏 is the simplified form of the character 詠. They are both pronounced *Yong* in Putonghua. The Chinese character 春 is pronounced as *Chun* in both Putonghua and Cantonese. The correct pronunciation for 詠春 and 咏春 is *Yong Chun* in Putonghua and *Wing Chun* in Cantonese.

Yong Chun and *Yong Chun Gong Fu* may well be the official terms as 咏春 or 詠春 gains popularity in Mainland China, but in keeping with the current preference, we here employ *Wing Chun* and *Wing Chun Kung Fu*.

The Origin of Wing Chun

Wing Chun was named after a beautiful young woman named Yim Wing-chun (嚴詠春) (Cantonese; Yan Yongchun in Putonghua). Supremely dazzling, she sold beancurd for a living and was nicknamed Doufu Xishi (豆腐西施) after Xishi, one of the four legendary maidens of ancient China. According to tradition, *Wing Chun*'s origin dates back approximately 250 years, to the reign of Emperor Qianlong (乾隆, 1736-1795).

Wu Mei (Ng Mui, 五枚), a Shaolin (少林) nun, took Yim Wing-chun under her protection, teaching her Shaolin *Kung Fu* in order to fend off the advances of an unwelcome suitor. Subsequently, Yim had a vision in the garden in which she observed a white crane and a snake fighting. Yim's epiphany inspired Wu Mei to found a new and revolutionary martial art, which she named after its originator: *Wing Chun Kung Fu*.

The new system was practiced in secret and passed down from generation to generation to a handful of chosen disciples. It remained relatively unknown until it reached Foshan, a city west of Guangzhou, where Liang Zan (梁贊), Grandmaster of the Fourth Generation, established its reputation by triumphing in numerous fights against opponents using conventional systems of *Kung Fu*.

It was Yip Man, the grand disciple of Liang Zan, who introduced the art to Hong Kong in 1949 when he escaped from Communist China. He is considered the founder of *Wing Chun Kung Fu* in Hong Kong (somewhat controversially; Liang Bi 梁璧, son of Liang Zan, taught Yip Man in Hong Kong).

Finally, Li Xiaolong (李小龍), known to the world as Bruce Lee, made *Wing Chun* famous in the 1960s and 1970s through his movies.

Wing Chun is Unique

Wing Chun Kung Fu is a relatively new and revolutionary martial art. It differs from other systems in forms, in its offensive and defensive concepts, and in its economy of power.

In more conventional martial arts systems, the various movements in the sequence of its forms are already fighting techniques; therefore, there are practical limits to the number of techniques which can be employed. The creation of a single new movement or fighting technique changes the entire sequence of its forms. Theoretically, by changing a movement in the sequence of a form alone, a new system can be founded. This has led to the proliferation of 'systems' – over 4000 of them in *Kung Fu*.

Wing Chun Kung Fu has three basic forms: primary, secondary and advanced. Unlike other martial arts systems, each movement in the sequence of each of its forms is not, by itself, a fighting technique. To give an analogy, individual movements in the sequence of *Wing Chun* forms can be equated to letters of the alphabet. Just as single letters do not typically form a word, so two or more movements are needed to form a fighting technique. However, just as there are countless words which can be formed by different permutations of the alphabet, so there is no limit to the number of fighting techniques which can be created by different combinations of movements in *Wing Chun*.

Thus, fighting techniques in *Wing Chun*:

Change according to the approach of the opponent.

In actual combat, *Wing Chun* emphasizes:

Nullifying attack while simultaneously counter-attacking.

Its concept of power is:

Diverting and utilizing the opponent's power.

Wing Chun Kung Fu is simple, direct and effective. As a result, over the past several decades *Wing Chun* has become one of the most popular and practiced martial arts in the world, in the process winning as adherents many established practitioners of other systems.

FAMILY TREE
(Hong Kong version)

The Hong Kong version of the *Wing Chun* family tree is incomplete. Therefore, we only include individuals mentioned in this book.

Wu Mei, a nun from the Shaolin Temple during the reign of Emperor Qianlong, initially taught Yim Wing-chun (Yan Yongchun) Shaolin *Kung Fu*. As a result of Wing-chun's vision of the battle between a white crane and a snake, Wu Mei founded a new system of *Kung Fu*, which she passed on to her disciple. Yim Wing-chun, who lent her name to the new martial art, taught her husband, Liang Bo-shau. Together, husband and wife were the First Generation.

They taught Liang Lan-gui (no relation). He was the Second Generation.

Liang Lan-gui taught Huang Hua-bao who exchanged his *Wing Chun* knowledge for the knowledge of Liang Er-di's *Six and A Half Point Pole*. They became the Third Generation.

Liang Er-di taught Liang Zan (no relation). Liang Zan earned the title *Mr Zan of Foshan* as a result of his proficiency. He was the Grandmaster (掌門人 *zhang men ren*) of the Fourth Generation.

The most prominent disciple of Liang Zan was Chen Hua-shun, who became the Grandmaster of the Fifth Generation.

Chen Hua-shun had 16 disciples. When he was over 70 years of age, he accepted Yip Man as his last disciple. Wu Zhong-su, his second disciple, taught Yip Man in Foshan. Liang Bi, son of

Liang Zan, taught Yip in Hong Kong. Chen Ru-mian (陳汝棉), son of Chen Hua-shun, became the Grandmaster of the Sixth Generation.

Yip Man was reputed to be the best of the Sixth Generation. He began to teach in Hong Kong beginning in 1949. His students and a handful of disciples from the 1950s, including the late Liang Xiang, Zhao Yun, Ye Bu-qing, Huang Chun-liang and Bruce Lee, undertook the responsibility of fighting proponents of other systems in order to gain recognition for *Wing Chun*. Duncan Leung is probably one of the most notable *Wing Chun* fighters of that period alive today.

Wu Mei 五枚
Founder

|

Yan Yongchun (Yim Wing-chun) 嚴詠春, Liang Bo-shau 梁博儔
First Generation

|

Liang Lan-gui 梁蘭桂
Second Generation

|

Huang Hua-bao 黃華寶, Liang Er-di 梁二娣
Third Generation

|

Liang Zan 梁贊*
Fourth Generation

|

Chen Hua-shun 陳華順*, Liang Bi 梁璧
Fifth Generation

|

Wu Zhong-su 吳仲素, Ye Wen (Yip Man) 葉問
Sixth Generation

|

Liang Xiang 梁相, Zhou Yun 招允, Ye Bo-qing 葉步青,
Huang Chun-liang 黃淳樑, Li Xiao-long (Bruce Lee) 李小龍,
Xu Shang-tian 徐尚田, Luo Yao 駱耀,
William Cheung 張卓慶, Zhang Xue-jian 張學健,
Liang Shao-hong (Duncan Leung) 梁紹鴻
Seventh Generation
(1950s)

|

Li Ying-jiu (Guy Lai) 黎應就, Liang Ting (Leung Ting) 梁挺
Eighth Generation

*Grandmaster of the generation

Family Tree

(Foshan version)

It is noteworthy that the names of Wu Mei and Yim Wing-chun are both absent from the Foshan version of the *Wing Chun* family tree. We cannot account for this discrepancy.

Ye Chen An Zhu, the First Generation, was a 22nd generation monk of Shaolin Temple in Songshan (嵩山), Henan Province (河南省). He lived in the period between the reigns of Emperor Yongzheng (雍正, 1723-1735) and Emperor Qianlong (1736-1795). When he retired to Hengshan (衡山), Hunan Province (湖南省), he taught Zhang Wu, a *Kung Fu* actor in *Yueju* (粵劇, Cantonese opera).

Zhang Wu, the Second Generation, taught Huang Hua-bao and Liang Er-di. They too were *Kung Fu* actors in *Yueju*.

They taught Liang Zan in Foshan, who became the Grandmaster of the Fourth Generation.

Liang Zan taught Chen Hua-shun, Liang Bi and others. Chen became the Grandmaster of the Fifth Generation.

Chen Hua-shun taught his son, Chen Ru-mian, who became the Grandmaster of the Sixth Generation, Wu Zhon-xu, Zhao Jiu, Ye Wen (Yip Man), and others.

Chen Ru-mian moved to Wuzhou (梧州), Guangxi Province (廣西省) in 1932 and taught there. His son, Chen Jia-shen, became the Grandmaster of the Seventh Generation, while his grandson, Chen Guo-ji, became the Grandmaster of the Eighth Generation.

Ye Chen An Zhu 一塵庵主
First Generation

|

Zhang Wu 張五
Second Generation

|

Huang Hua-bao 黃華寶, Liang Er-di 梁二娣
Third Generation

|

Liang Zan 梁贊*
Fourth Generation

|

Chen Hua-shun 陳華順*, Liang Bi 梁璧
Fifth Generation

|

Wu Zhong-su 吳仲素, Chen Ru-mian 陳汝棉*,
Zhao Jia 招就, Ye Wen (Yip Man) 葉問
Sixth Generation

|

Chen Jia-shen 陳家桑*, Chen Jia-lian 陳家廉
Seventh Generation

|

Chen Guo-ji 陳國基*
Eighth Generation

*Grandmaster of the generation

PART ONE

實 踐 武 功

Applied Kung Fu

Application is the only way to verify the truth
實 踐 是 抵 達 真 理 的 唯 一 途 徑
(*shi jian shi di da zhen li di wei yi yu jing*)
Buddha (c. 500 B.C.)

There are, perhaps, over 4000 styles and systems of *Kung Fu*, and it is said that all of these can be traced, directly or indirectly, to the Shaolin Temple. From one point of view, they can be categorized as either performing art or applied fighting art.

Fighting techniques and theories which have not been rigorously tested under actual fighting conditions – and whose martial effectiveness is therefore questionable – would be classified as performing arts. The techniques may be difficult to perform and spectacular to watch, but they cannot be deployed in combat. There is a marked tendency for practitioners of performance art to spar verbally, each boasting of the superiority of his particular style; this seems to take the place of actual physical encounters.

Applied fighting arts are fighting techniques and theories which have been proven over time in genuine combat. The techniques are often simple to perform and not particularly elegant as theatre, but they are deployable by anyone who cares to learn. Applied martial artists have the innate confidence to allow their fighting skills to represent them: they do not need to tout.

Kung Fu (功夫), a Cantonese term, has in the past several decades come to be the most common name for Chinese martial arts, while *Wugong* (武功) is the most appropriate term for actual fighting ability. *Wugong* is *Kung Fu* (功夫) plus *Gongli* (功力). *Gongli* is the art of exerting power to knock down an opponent. Without *Gongli*, a practitioner's fighting ability or *Wugong* is limited. A *Wugong* practitioner applies his fighting techniques and theories in practice – genuine combat – and only after accumulating extensive fighting experience can his *Wugong* be considered as applied art.

There are millions of *Kung Fu* practitioners in China, yet there has not been a single convincing fighter from China in the past several decades. Since the establishment of the People's Republic of China in October 1949, Chinese citizens have been prohibited from studying *Kung Fu* for combat, because the government wanted to dispel competition and infighting among rival schools.

As a result, *Kung Fu* has been relegated to exercise and the stage. Over the past 50 years China has produced many *Kung Fu* performers but not a single genuine *Kung Fu* fighter. As *Kung Fu* techniques have become more complicated to perform and more spectacular to watch, Chinese competitors have won countless gold medals in *Wushu* (武術) and *Kung Fu* performing events in the Asian Games. However, they simply do not have fighting experience, and it is doubtful that their *Wugong* could be effectively applied in real combat situations.

Among the refugees fleeing China after the Revolution were many outstanding martial artists. They gathered in Hong Kong, opened *Kung Fu* studios and taught their respective styles to eke out a living. Towering above this group of expatriate martial arts instructors was Yip Man of Foshan, whose student Bruce Lee went on to popularize *Kung Fu* internationally. Bruce Lee eventually mixed the *Wing Chun Kung Fu* he learned from Yip Man with elements of other Chinese and foreign martial arts to found *Jeet Kune Do* (截拳道). After his untimely death, Bruce Lee became even more popular than during his lifetime. However, it was *Wing Chun*, rather than *Jeet Kune Do*, which benefited from his posthumous fame. Yip Man was elevated to the zenith of his career. *Wing Chun* spread to the four corners of the globe and almost became synonymous with *Kung Fu*.

In spite of its popularity and large number of adherents, today there are few noteworthy *Wing Chun* fighters. The reason lies in the distinction between performance and applied art. However, there is a glimmer of hope that one or more worthy *Wing Chun* fighters will arise when and if the *Wing Chun Warrior* passes on his knowledge of Applied *Wing Chun* to future generations.

Chapter 1

THE PROFESSOR HUMBLED

Virginia Beach
1993

Frog in the well
井 底 之 蛙
(jing di zhi wa)
Zhuangzi (莊子, 350-286 B.C.)

Zhuangzi was a Taoist philosopher of the Warring States Period (475-221 B.C.), who used fables, often humorous, to convey moral lessons. He was the foremost spiritual descendant of Laozi (老子), founder of Taoism. *Frog In The Well* is Zhuangzi's well known tale which cautions against imposing our limited perspectives upon life. 'Are you aware', Zhuangzi seems to ask, 'of the limitations imposed by our own ignorance?'

Listen to the narrative of Professor Li Hon-ki, told in his own words, about his encounter with Duncan Leung:

I have been a martial arts fanatic since my teens. I have studied a number of systems, including various styles of *Kung Fu*. In 1965, when I was 13, I began to learn *Zhou Jia* (周家) and *Hong Quan* (洪拳).

By 1968, Bruce Lee had made *Wing Chun* world famous, and

like many of my contemporaries, I plunged into it with enthusiasm. For the next three years I learned from a *Wing Chun* instructor of the Seventh Generation. I worked hard and attained the level to manipulate the Wooden Man, Double Knives and Long Pole. But, I felt something was missing. Between 1971 and 1973, I studied under three more *Wing Chun* instructors, also of the Seventh Generation, ensuring that I learned everything there was to learn. During this period I also learned *Tai Ji Quan* (太極拳), *Tae Kwon Do* and *Karate*. Suffice to say, I was versatile.

In 1973, I won the Hong Kong *Tae Kwon Do* Open Championship. In 1977, I was the runner-up in the Hong Kong *Kung Fu* Association Competition. I was confident in my abilities and quite proud of myself.

In June 1979 I left Hong Kong for Brazil and started teaching *Kung Fu* there. I taught *Hong Quan, Tai Ji Quan* and *Wing Chun*. It didn't take long for me to become an established instructor. In addition, I continued my own learning.

My major problem was against kicks. Thai Boxing is well known for its ferocious and crippling kicks. Without special training to strengthen my legs, I could not even stand if a Thai boxer landed a kick on any part of my legs. At that time, I felt it necessary to learn the Thai way because *Wing Chun* had hardly any kicks or the training to strengthen the lower limbs. Later, I would find out how wrong this notion was.

Oyama Karate was popular in Brazil, and like practitioners of other martial arts systems and *Kung Fu* styles, these people had to learn the Thai way of kicking in order to stand any chance against Thai boxers. I learned the techniques from an *Oyama Karate* practitioner who came to me to study *Wing Chun*.

For the next five years, I practiced until I could break a two-by-four when it was smashed against my shins. I could withstand any kick to my legs from any style or system. I was inordinately proud of my achievement, something, I felt, few *Wing Chun* practitioners could match.

In 1993, the financial crisis in Brazil compelled me to leave São Paulo for New York City. For the next two years I ran a clinic of Chinese traditional medicine there, and business flourished.

That year, I was invited to demonstrate at the World *Kung Fu* Championships in San Francisco. What could be more gratifying for my ego than to show off the prowess of my kicks before the world? Before a huge audience and with massive television coverage, with my assistants firmly holding a baseball bat perpendicular to the floor, with a single kick I broke it in half with my left shin. Not a bad demonstration of kicking ability.

However, there was one person I respected who was impressed with neither my prowess nor my *Kung Fu* – my older brother Albert. He suggested I should meet an old friend of his in Virginia. For years he had been telling me about Duncan Leung and how masterful was his martial art ability. Frankly, I was tired of hearing about this guy. So what if he was Seventh Generation *Wing Chun*? I had learned from not one but four experts of the Seventh Generation. What more could anyone teach me? Finally, worn down by my brother's persistence, but very skeptical, I traveled with him somewhat reluctantly to Virginia Beach, a resort city on the Virginia coastline.

We were invited as guests at Duncan's home. The day after our arrival, I accompanied Duncan not to his *Kung Fu* studio, which was the object of my visit, but to his office, hanging around from 9:00 in the morning until 5:30 in the afternoon. Whenever I mentioned *Wing Chun*, he changed the subject. I was very annoyed. After all, I had come all the way from New York City on martial arts business, and here he would not even discuss the topic.

Duncan sensed my frustration. "What do you want?" he asked.

"My brother told me you are a *Wing Chun* expert, and I want to see what you know." Duncan didn't seem very interested.

"What have you learned?"

"I have learned everything, Wooden Man, Double Knives and Long Pole."

"You have learned everything. There is nothing more I can teach you."

"Why don't we *Chi Sau*?" I challenged him.

Chi Sau (黐手) is a drill, unique to *Wing Chun*, in which practitioners improve their sensitivity in contact with an opponent. The most important aspect of *Chi Sau* trains the practitioner to cover exposed areas. It is not a technique and therefore it cannot be used for fighting. This is a serious misconception even among many *Wing Chun* instructors.

I was more than proud of my *Chi Sau*. I had yet to encounter another *Wing Chun* artist who could beat me at it. Duncan could see how eager I was to flaunt my *Chi Sau* expertise, and he decided to give me the opportunity to show off.

He arose from his chair. Walking to the front of his desk, he beckoned me to likewise stand up. I got up from my chair and walked to the front of his desk. As soon as we intertwined our forearms, I knew I was beaten. His forearms clung to mine like intertwined snakes! In vain I pulled and pushed, sensing nothing! Where was my sensory perception? Duncan looked as if he was in a trance. There was a settee behind me in the office, and whenever I tried to exert power to pull and push, I was ignominiously bounced back onto the settee. Duncan betrayed no sense of triumph; in fact, he appeared completely indifferent, except that he must have felt sorry for my students back in Brazil!

Wouldn't you think that being dumped three times should be enough to convince me that I had met my master? Not yet – I was stubborn. I still had powerful kicks in my arsenal of tricks.

"Duncan, your *Chi Sau* is amazing. Now I know what *Chi Sau* really is."

"Forget it. I am sure there are other guys who are better than I am."

"I know *Wing Chun* has hardly any kicks. Can you stop my kicks?"

"You are right. *Wing Chun* has hardly any kicks. The feet are not for kicking. They are for breaking."

"What do you mean?"

"One of the most difficult techniques of *Wing Chun* is to master the skills of kicking. *Wing Chun* kicks are powerful and they break legs."

"I don't believe it. Try me." I should have realized that I was asking for trouble, but I had to show him the prowess of my kicks.

"I tell you what. I am going to break your leg if you try to kick me."

"No way!" I would be in my element. My shins were my showpiece. They broke baseball bats.

I moved into my combative stance, while Duncan just stood there calmly with his arms behind his back (just as he had witnessed his *Sifu* do in Hong Kong in 1955 when facing a challenger – see Chapter 12). The moment I swung my mighty left foot at him, his right foot was already there to meet the inside of my left knee! He just tapped it, and my balance was gone. I knew he could easily have snapped it.

"I want you to be my *Sifu*. Please accept me," I humbly entreated.

"No way. I cannot accept you."

I knew it was my overt arrogance that had hardened him against me. I began to plead with Duncan, but his reply was still negative.

"Anyway, you live too far away."

Nor could my brother Albert change Duncan's mind. We left Virginia Beach and returned to New York City. I felt very sorry for myself. All the years of hard work studying *Wing Chun* were worthless. What had I learned? Duncan should have broken my knee, forcing me to kneel before him in crippled supplication. Maybe then he would have accepted me out of sympathy.

I pondered the last line of Duncan's refusal: "You live too far away," and wondered whether this was my salvation. That was it! I was going to live so close to him that he had no excuse to turn me down.

Determined, I went to see Ma Man Nam, Duncan's first disciple (see Chapter 25), seeking his advice. He told me about the special *Sifu Worship Ceremony* (拜師儀式 – see Chapter 6) and taught me how to prepare. I closed my busy medical practice and, with the blessing of Albert, I left New York City for Virginia Beach.

Two months after our initial encounter, Duncan opened the front door of his home to find me standing there holding two suitcases. He was shocked. But he realized the depths of my determination and acceded to my request. After years of searching, I had finally found my master.

The *Sifu Worship Ceremony* was traditional. Having been coached by Ma Man Nam, I brought joss sticks, rice wine, tiny porcelain cups, a pewter urn, roast pork, the *bi shi tie* (拜師帖) and the red packet. After the mandatory *three kneels nine kowtows*, I became a disciple of the Eighth Generation. Duncan Leung became my *Sifu*.

When I went the first time to his studio, I saw his students and disciples sparring among themselves, and I was anxious to participate. But *Sifu* told me I had no chance against them. To satisfy my curiosity, he asked a 15-year-old boy to spar with me. *Sifu* was right. I could not stand his bombardment because I did not know how to *cover*. I was even more demoralized when he told me the boy had been with him for only nine months! But he told me that after a year of intensive training I should be much better than they were because I had a sound foundation.

For the next two years I worked and learned under *Sifu's* guidance; the training was indeed intensive. Everything he taught was so different from the *Wing Chun* I had learned before. I was learning *Applied Wing Chun*.

Toward the end of 1994, I returned to Brazil, and for the first time in my life, inwardly I felt like a man. *Sifu* did not merely teach me self-defense. From him I developed true self-confidence and self-esteem. In fact, the credo of Duncan Leung's *Wing Chun* Academy is *Confidence, Defense, Esteem*.

Not surprisingly, just as my *Sifu* had been, I was ridiculed by other teachers who said that what I was teaching was not *Wing Chun*. But I could forgive their ignorance, for I had once been among them, until fortune showed me the error of my ways.

KIAI Kung Fu Magazine was the most popular martial arts publication at that time. The magazine asked to interview me, and that interview would change my life. The subjects discussed included *Kung Fu*, traditional Chinese medicine – which includes the art of diagnosis, acupuncture, and herbal medicines – and

Oriental philosophy. During the course of the interview, I also issued an open challenge to martial artists and *Kung Fu* practitioners, particularly *Wing Chun* skeptics.

The interview caught the attention of the administrators of UNEB, the State University of Bahia, Brazil, who then invited me to teach *Applied Wing Chun* at that institution. Later I would work with the university in researching herbal medicines. In 1996, I was invited to the chair of Professorship in Chinese Traditional Medicine and Oriental Studies. Since then, I have been teaching acupuncture, herbal medicines, massage, *Qi Gong* (氣功) and Oriental Studies in UNEB in Bahia and at branches of the university in São Paulo and Rio de Janeiro.

My students were winners at the 1996 World *Wushu* Championships in Zhengzhou (鄭州), Henan Province (河南省), China, and at the 1998 World *Guoshu* Championships in Taipei. Currently, I serve as Consultant and Chief Instructor for the *Kung Fu* Federation of Brazil, and Director and Chief Instructor of the Olympic *Wushu* Committee of Chile.

I continue to visit *Sifu* and learn from him whenever possible, usually in the summers. I now realize that there is still so much to learn from him, and I only wish I had the time to study more. As a token of my esteem for *Sifu*, I teach *Applied Wing Chun*. If I have to use one word to describe my *Sifu*'s *Applied Wing Chun*, it is: unfathomable!

Professor Li is not ashamed to admit the truth – he wasted decades learning, practicing, and flaunting a martial arts knowledge that simply did not work when it came to practical application. He now freely confesses that he was a 'frog in the well admiring his own croak'. He counts himself fortunate to have finally met a true master – in his opinion an undisputed *Applied Wing Chun* genius.

Professor Li hopes that his story will serve as a cautionary tale to other frogs. He considers himself lucky to have *only* wasted 28 years! There are many who have unknowingly spent a lifetime learning and even teaching something that is useless in practice. Li hopes that they will one day discover, as he did, that 'the sky is so much bigger than the mouth of the well, and one's croak is audible only to oneself'.

Professor Li broke the baseball bat in half with his left shin

Chapter 2

PURE WING CHUN

New York
1974

Those who know don't say
Those who say don't know
知 者 不 言 言 者 不 知
(zhi zhe bu yan, yan zhe bu zhi)
The Classic of the Virtue of the Tao (道德經)
Laozi (老子)

Laozi, whose profound philosophy became a world religion – Taoism – lived during the Spring and Autumn Period (770-474 B.C.). He was born before Confucius (551-479 B.C.), but the biographic details of Laozi's life are obscured. The place and manner of his death are likewise unknown.

The ludicrous conceit of the King of Yilang is an idiom which refers to people who boast plenty while knowing little. It was written by the renowned historian Sima Qian (司馬遷) in his *Records of the Historian*. The king of Yilang, a tiny country during the Han Dynasty (206 B.C.- 220 A.D.), bragged about the extent and wealth of his kingdom when in reality it was only the size of a town in the Han Empire.

Duncan's first studio, at No.3 Great Jones Street, was in one of the least desirable neighborhoods on the fringe of New York's Chinatown. But the rent was cheap, and there was ample space in which to teach and practice.

The fellows from the NYPD (see Chapter 22) were true to their word. They came to learn and referred not only their colleagues but also friends and relatives. Duncan's business got a rapid jump-start.

One day, Duncan was teaching a group of students when a Chinese man in his forties, wearing a *chang shan* – 長衫, a traditional Chinese male long robe – walked into the studio followed by a retinue of about five young men, all wearing white T-shirts and black *Kung Fu* trousers.

The leader looked around, trying to figure out who was the instructor.

"I am X *Sifu*. Who is Duncan Leung?"

"I am."

"You are Leung *Sifu*?" Appraising Duncan, he was surprised to find a man appearing to be in his early twenties. Though 32 at the time, Duncan appeared much younger than his actual age. Apparently, he did not look like *Sifu* material.

The man said: "I am Yip Man's eldest disciple." (He meant in the United States).

"Then you are my elder *Kung Fu* brother."

"Now that you are teaching *Wing Chun* I would like to invite you to join the *Wing Chun Kung Fu* Federation."

"Sure. It would be nice to meet *Wing Chun* brothers."

"Here is my address in Brooklyn. There will be a meeting on Wednesday. Please make an effort to come." He handed Duncan his business card, and departed.

On the day of the meeting, Duncan, together with his disciple Ma Man Nam and a couple of other students, arrived at the address in Brooklyn. The studio had many rooms, including a 'challenging' room. Duncan spied a Wooden Man in one of the rooms and went over to inspect it.

"Don't touch it! It belongs to my *Sifu*. Nobody is allowed to touch it without his permission." One of the students was actually serious about this.

"OK, I won't touch it. No big deal." Duncan couldn't help but adding: "In any case, the arms of the Wooden Man are not in the right places."

After everyone had gathered around the conference room table, X *Sifu* introduced Duncan: "This is Leung *Sifu*. He says he has learned from Yip Man."

His words and tone made it obvious that he was doubting Duncan in front of his followers.

"Let me make it clear. We are very democratic. We observe tradition and respect our elders. Seniority is important and therefore the chairmanship always goes to the most senior. It is not elected. I am the most senior in North America and I have been the chairman ever since." X *Sifu* was obviously keen to be the chairman. "The North American *Kung Fu* Federation has invited *Wing Chun* to give demonstrations."

As he uttered the last word, he looked straight at Duncan who responded: "I am new in town and have only just started teaching. I don't know what to do. If there is anything I can do to help, please let me know."

"Leung *Sifu*, it is strange that you have claimed you are Yip Man's disciple. I am the most senior here. I was with Yip Man the longest. How come I never saw you at Yip Man's studio?" His statement was not unprepared. In fact, it had obviously been rehearsed.

Duncan asked: "When did you start learning from *Sifu*?"

"1–9–6–4." Each number was uttered slowly and deliberately in a manner calculated to show off his early attendance.

"That would explain it. I completed my private tuition in 1959, when I left for Australia. No wonder we have never met."

This bombshell was unexpected. Now his facial expression changed.

"In that case, I should call you *Sihing* (師兄, elder *Kung Fu* brother), and you should be the chairman," he reluctantly offered.

"Firstly, I don't want to be the chairman," said Duncan. "I am new in town and I don't even know which way is north and south. Secondly, teaching *Kung Fu* is not my career. It is a temporary measure. Thirdly, you are a good organizer, and you have been the chairman for so long. You are the natural choice. It doesn't really matter who is more senior. You are older than I am, and I have no problem addressing you as *Sihing*."

X *Sifu* insisted and Duncan resisted, but when the meeting eventually broke up, the atmosphere was friendly, and X *Sifu* remained the chairman.

One day, a year later, Duncan retuned to his studio after lunch to find it totally empty. Not a single student was there. Wondering where everybody had gone, Duncan picked up a newspaper and started reading. Just then, Ma Man Nam came charging in with a couple of students, exclaiming: "*Sifu,* there is trouble!"

"Where is everybody?" Duncan enquired.

"They all left for X *Sifu*'s studio."

"What for?"

"They read this in the newspaper and went there to fight for justice." He pointed to an ad:

正宗詠春 (*jin chong yong chun*)
Our Studio Teaches <u>PURE</u> Wing Chun!

Duncan understood immediately why his students were furious. They had every reason to be. The advertisement insinuated that what they were learning was less than pure *Wing Chun*. He jumped up to go to X *Sifu's* studio to stop this futile dispute before it got out of hand.

By the time Duncan arrived, the two groups of students were pointing fingers and arguing vociferously. X *Sifu* sat quietly in his armchair, doing nothing to defuse the volatile situation. He seemed to be curious about what Duncan might do.

Duncan interrupted the argument by shouting to his students: "Stop arguing. Who cares whose *Wing Chun* is pure or not? What a waste of time. Let's go back to the studio."

Reluctantly, the students turned toward the door, feeling defeated. Their egos were hurt, wondering why their *Sifu* did not even defend them. Their bewilderment and suffering pained Duncan. He felt that they must be wondering whether there was a grain of truth in the advertisement.

Seeing that Duncan was not in a confrontational mood, X *Sifu* got up and started lecturing the students, his and Duncan's, about pure *Wing Chun*.

"Come on, stop this lecturing. It is a waste of time," Duncan told him.

"No, it is not a waste of time. The younger generations need to know what pure *Wing Chun* is. I have to teach them that there is *sky beyond sky* (天外有天 *tian wai you tian*, there is always something and someone better)."

For Duncan, this was the proverbial straw that broke the camel's back. This he finally took as an insult, particularly in front of his students. He stood before X *Sifu*, pointing his right index finger at him: "X, what are you teaching now? If you are so good, let's fight. If I lose I will take my shingle down, and if you lose you take down yours. You are no match for me! *I will even tie my legs together and tie one of my arms against my body. I will beat you with one arm!*" In his anger, Duncan had issued a challenge that could not be refused.

Or could it? X *Sifu* refused. "To avoid disharmony between brothers," he announced, "from now on I am teaching a new *Kung Fu* system. It is X *Kung Fu*." Thereafter, he took his *Wing Chun* shingle down!

Out of consideration for a fellow martial artist, Duncan Leung will not identify X Sifu.

Chapter 3

APPLIED WING CHUN

Hong Kong
2001

When the unreal is taken for real, the real becomes unreal
假 作 真 時 真 亦 假
(*jia zou zhen shi zhen yi jia*)
Dream of the Red Chamber (紅樓夢)
Cao Xue-qin (曹雪芹, 1715-1763)

In *Dream of the Red Chamber*, one of the four classical Chinese novels, Cao Xue-qin, famous Qing Dynasty author, commented that when the masses are convinced that the unreal is real, even the real will be rejected as unreal because it has no relation to their illusion.

Similarly, the majority of *Wing Chun Kung Fu* practitioners have never seen, much less practiced, genuine fighting techniques and theory. Hence they do not recognize Duncan Leung's *Applied Wing Chun* for what it is.

White cat or black cat, whichever catches mice is a good cat
— Deng Xiaoping (鄧小平)
Pure or impure Wing Chun, whatever beats an opponent is good Wing Chun — Duncan Leung (梁紹鴻)

Deng Xiaoping, the single individual most responsible for propelling China into the modern world, was the architect of 'Socialism with Chinese Characteristics'. This approach has transformed China with stunning rapidity since 1978 from a backward, underdeveloped communist country into an emerging superpower possessing upward mobility, prosperity, and the respect of the world. His now well-known *white cat / black cat* epigram epitomizes a pragmatic approach to life, including the practical application of any program or system – whether it be socialism or *Wing Chun Kung Fu*.

Duncan Leung is a believer in the effective application of the *Wing Chun Kung Fu* he learned from his *Sifu*. He believes the over-used adjectives – such as *authentic, practical, pure, superior* or *ultimate* – tend to be misleading. Unless students can prove to themselves that what they have learned actually works in practice, this knowledge is useless. After having observed *Wing Chun* under all manner of conditions – on the street, in studios, at testimonials – Duncan has come to the conclusion that there are two types of *Wing Chun*. One kind is academic; intellectual knowledge which is of little practical value. The other prepares one for fighting, enabling one to overcome an opponent in actual combat.

Duncan calls *Wing Chun* that can be utilized in real combat *Applied Wing Chun*.

At Duncan's seminars, participants with a background in *Kung Fu* and/or *Wing Chun* often ask him why he does not teach them *Wing Chun*. The techniques and methods Duncan teaches are new and unfamiliar to them. But their eyes are opened when they discover they cannot even *cover* a single swing. (However, Duncan is able to show students in about 15 minutes how simple it really is to *cover* a swing, no matter how powerful!)

Duncan explains: "What I can do is not important. It is only important that you can do what I show you. If I cannot teach you, what use am I? In science, it is not what can be done once that is significant, but what can be replicated."

There was an abacus expert who claimed his mathematics was the best in the village. He was absolutely right. His mathematics was authentic and of the purest lineage because he had learned it from his father, who in turn had learned from his father, and so on back through the generations. It was a family secret. His efficiency and expertise in the use of an abacus was beyond compare. He could add, subtract, multiply and divide, even blindfolded. Everybody wanted to learn from him.

One day, one of his students told him of something he had witnessed in the city. His cousin was learning mathematics from an expert who used ABC and XYZ. When the student from the village informed the city mathematician that he wasn't teaching pure and authentic mathematics, the mathematician agreed with him totally. The villager felt superior to his cousin because he had the unique good fortune to learn pure and authentic mathematics from his teacher with the impeccable lineage. What he did not realize was that he had witnessed algebra, a subject of which his teacher was entirely ignorant. (The postscript to the story is that the abacus expert had the good sense to send his own children to the city to learn algebra.)

Duncan Leung's advice on seeking an instructor

Beware of people who drape themselves in mystique. To protect yourself is a birthright, and to learn *Kung Fu* is to exercise that right. In other words, this is a natural function and there is nothing mysterious or esoteric about the practice.

Beware of those who ask you to be overly patient. They either don't know themselves, or they are stringing the student along in order to extract more money. A decent instructor should be able to teach you how to protect yourself within a reasonably short period of time. However, those with little or no fighting experience cannot teach others.

Duncan knew an unscrupulous instructor who himself had learned nothing more than *siu nim tau* – the elementary *Wing Chun* (see Chapter 11). This individual sold videotapes of *Wing Chun* movements he simply made up, while claiming his version was superior because he had inherited a secret *Wing Chun* menu. His unsuspecting students never learned or practiced beyond *siu nim tau*. In addition, he convinced them to learn his version of *Qi Gong* (氣功) for accumulating internal power. They were even guaranteed that after five years they would be able to floor an opponent with one punch, without physical contact, and were told that if they were not careful, they might even kill him!

Those who were impatient left after a while. Those who were patient and loyal also left, but it took them much longer, and by the time they suspected the truth, they had spent thousands. Students came and went; they ultimately left in disappointment and disgust, but the instructor laughed all the way to the bank.

Duncan denies any personal knowledge of *Qi Gong*, although he sometimes recommends *Tai Ji Quan* and hatha yoga for their health benefits. He says: "I must admit I don't know *Qi Gong*, and I am therefore not qualified to say anything for or against it. I am sure *Qi Gong* is useful in many ways. But relating it to impossible feats is irresponsible and misleading." (*Qi Gong* fever subsided even more rapidly in the 1990s than acupuncture fever in the 1970s, when a couple of renowned *Qi Gong* artists were caught red-handed by hidden cameras, and their incredible feats were revealed to be inferior illusions.)

There is a story told that when the magician David Copperfield was in Beijing he was introduced to a famous *Qi Gong* specialist. It was before his incredible feat of walking through the Great Wall of China with worldwide television coverage. He asked the specialist to show him his *Qi Gong*. The reply was, "Your *Qi Gong* is better than mine!"

On The Subject Of Lineage

Martial artistry, like skill in painting, music and literature, is not genetically inherited. There is no Picasso II, Son of Chopin, or William Shakespeare, Jr.

Looking at the *Wing Chun* family tree, one notices that the most prominent in each succeeding generation is not related to the previous generation's greatest achiever. Among the many Liangs, none were related except Liang Zan and his son Liang Bi, who taught Yip Man in Hong Kong.

Even so, in the Fifth Generation, Liang Bi was not the most outstanding *Wing Chun* proponent. He was overshadowed by Chen Hua-shun, a disciple of his father. The fact that Yip Man was better than his contemporaries when he returned to Foshan led to speculation that there were secret menus passed from Liang Zan to Liang Bi. Speculation that secret menus passed from Yip Man to his two offspring remains highly suspect.

Wing Chun In Decline

Bruce Lee is, arguably, still the most famous Chinese in the world, loved and admired for his amazing *Kung Fu* more than 30 years after his death. It is due to his continuing popularity that *Wing*

Chun Kung Fu and Yip Man have also achieved wide recognition.

Unfortunately, *Wing Chun*'s very popularity has attracted unscrupulous businessmen and mediocre instructors. Rather than teach an art form, certain individuals have infiltrated its ranks for pecuniary gain. Often they mystify the art in an attempt to mislead gullible students. Such individuals abuse the trust that is mistakenly placed in them.

Today Chinese *Kung Fu*, *Wing Chun* in particular, is derided because Chinese combatants are consistently demolished in free fight (散打) competition by Thai fighters and other martial arts practitioners. It is very sad to witness desperate Chinese *Kung Fu* combatants increasingly adopting the techniques and methods of Thai boxers and wrestlers.

PART TWO
1964–1973

武 德
(*Wu De*)

MARTIAL VIRTUES

A great warrior should possess wisdom (智 *zhi*),
credibility (信 *xin*), humanity (仁 *ren*), courage (勇 *yong*)
and severity (嚴 *yan*).
The Art of War (孫子兵法)
Sunzi (孫子, 500 B.C.)

Chivalry

The concept of chivalry was the ideal to which medieval
European knights aspired. It embodies the qualities of courage,
honor, courtesy, and concern for the weak and helpless.

Virtues

More difficult virtues were expected of Xiake (俠客) or Xiashi
(俠士), individuals adept in martial arts – swordsmen and *Kung
Fu* practitioners – in ancient China and in recent dynasties. Their
ideal qualities included chivalry, righteousness, humanity, integrity
and *yi qi* (義氣) which means loyalty to your friends, and personal
honour or commitment to your words. While the knights and

swordsmen of old may have passed into history, the virtues to which they aspired remain the goals for many martial artists.

Courage

Courage in the face of adversity is a rare quality possessed by few. Generosity of spirit, the willingness to give of one's time and experience, the effort to help the weak, the poor, and the helpless – these are within the reach of every individual. How many martial arts practitioners have the courage to step forward in time of need to stop injustice against the weak and to protect them physically when they are bullied? They have the means, but do they have the courage? To fight for justice and put one's life in jeopardy is the quality of people whom we call heroes, and these individuals are rare indeed.

Righteousness

Righteousness embodies the qualities of morality, justice, and decency.

Yi Qi (義氣)

In the English language, there exists no term that captures the quality of unwavering loyalty to your friends and commitment to your words. It is the kind of trust on which unshakeable friendship is founded: *At home rely on parents, away from home rely on friends* (在家靠父母 *zai jia kao fu mu*, 在外靠朋友 *zai wai kao peng you*). In olden times, some people would go so far as killing their own kin (大義滅親 *da yi mie qin*) to prove to their friends their loyalty, innocence or trustworthiness.

Lord Guan (關公 Guan Gong), in the classical Chinese novel *Romance of The Three Kingdoms,* was so renowned for his *yi qi* that he has been deified, especially by various brotherhoods such as policemen and triad members. In secret societies, betraying fellow members is considered the most heinous violation of the codes of honor. Slow and painful execution for this offense serves as a warning to others.

A legacy of loyalty close to four centuries

The following story is a testament to the virtue of *yi qi*. However unbelievable it may sound, for 17 generations the She (佘) clan has dedicated itself to guarding the tomb of a Ming Dynasty general. Defying persecution and family tragedy, since 1630 the members of this clan have demonstrated unwavering loyalty and commitment to a cause: *yi qi*.

General Yuan Chonghuan (袁崇煥, 1584–1630) was a native of Dongguan (東莞), a city south of Guangzhou. He successfully defended the northern frontier from repeated invasions by the Manchus during the 17th-century reign of Emperor Chongzhen (崇禎), the last Emperor of the Ming Dynasty (1368-1644).

The Manchus spread false rumors that General Yuan was in collaboration with them to overthrow the Ming Dynasty. Believing those rumors, Chongzhen had General Yuan arrested, and proclaimed him a traitor. His death sentence was carried out by public dismemberment – death by a thousand cuts (凌遲處死, *ling chi chu si*), one of the cruelest methods of execution.

A loyal follower collected General Yuan's remains, including his decapitated head, which he stole from the execution ground. He buried them and kept the location as a family secret, known only to his immediate kin. He vowed to protect it and pledged his descendants to do the same. To protect their identities, he and his descendants changed the family surname numerous times over the decades. The original family name was lost even as the promise was preserved: they continued to hide the location of the tomb.

Eventually, during the reign of Emperor Qianlong in the Qing Dynasty (1644-1911), General Yuan was given a posthumous royal pardon, and his valor was recognized. It had finally become safe to reveal the location of the tomb, which was in Beijing. During that period, the name of the clan had become She. The descendants of the She clan regarded it a singular honor to guard the tomb and members of their family resided alongside it for generations.

The tomb – and the promise – survived invasion by imperialists and colonialists during the final years of the Qing Dynasty, the Dynasty's fall in 1911, the warlord years during which the country was engulfed in civil war, the Japanese invasion and World War II, and finally the civil war between the Nationalists and the Communists.

When Mao Zedong (毛澤東) proclaimed the birth of the People's Republic of China in 1949, the tomb was officially designated a historical site. A proper tomb and an ancestral hall were constructed. But the She clan was not to live peacefully in the ancestral hall for long. During the Cultural Revolution between 1967 and 1977, the Red Guards went on a national rampage, destroying historical sites throughout China. While the tomb itself was fortunately spared because of its relative obscurity, a Red Guard leader ejected the She and installed himself in the ancestral hall, where he and his family continue to reside today. The She have been living in a tiny shack attached to the hall.

She You-zhi (佘幼芝) is the last direct descendant of General Yuan Chonghuan's loyal follower. Married to a teacher, Jiao Li-jiang (焦立江), she has a 28-year-old son, Jiao Ping. Supportive of the She family legacy and the commitment to guard the tomb,

She's husband has lived with her in the meager shack despite the opportunity for better housing as a teacher.

For the past 20 years, She You-zhi has lobbied the government in Beijing to renovate the tomb and ancestral hall. Finally, in 1992, the municipal government paid 50,000 yuan to erect a new memorial. There is hope that the Chinese People's Political Consultative Conference will rebuild the ancestral hall. The couple's son is willing to change his surname to She, so that he can follow in the footsteps of his ancestors and continue the sacred tradition of guarding the General's tomb.

Chapter 4

A Mysterious Old Man

Hong Kong
1964

Seeing what is right and not acting is cowardice
見 義 不 為 無 勇 也
(*jian yi bu wei wu yang ye*)
The Analects of Confucius (論語)
Confucius (孔子, 551-479 B.C.)

Confucius, of the Spring and Autumn Period (770-474 B.C.), is the best known Chinese philosopher. For thousands of years the ruling class embraced his teachings because he stressed *loyalty to the emperor and love of country*. To become a man of honor or a commendable person became the goals of literary and military men. The word *yi* (義) refers to honorable and commendable deeds.

Seeing what is right and acting courageously (見義勇為, *jian yi yang wei*), and *encountering injustice, draw a sword to help* (路見不平, *lu jian bu ping* 拔刀相助, *bu dao xiang zhu*) are folk idioms which remind us to come to the aid of people in distress.

Helping others is a virtue expected of every *Kung Fu* practitioner. Otherwise, why learn *Kung Fu* at all? The martial artist should be prepared to help the oppressed, the bullied, and the downtrodden. While as a philosophy the pen may be mightier than the sword, in certain instances, fists – judiciously used – are the only practical solution. Such was the case in the following incident involving Duncan Leung, *Wing Chun Warrior*.

Duncan and a friend were queuing for cinema tickets at the London Theatre in Kowloon, which was situated on the northwest junction of Nathan and Austin Roads. (The theatre has since been demolished and replaced by a modern building housing a cinema of the same name). Outside the theatre, illegal hawkers were busy selling preserved pickles, fruits, candies, roasted walnuts and other delicacies. The pavements were usually so crowded with people – ticket holders, pedestrians and hawkers – that one literally had to squeeze oneself through the mob of people to pass through.

On this particular day, there was a sudden eruption of yelling and cursing. People scattered in every direction to find the source of the commotion.

Two young hawkers, sellers of roasted squid, were ferociously beating an old man who appeared to be in his sixties. Their fists were raining down on him. Prostrate, he lay on the ground without moving. People in the crowd watched the beating, but nobody came to the old man's rescue. They didn't dare: everyone was deathly afraid of the triad's swift revenge. Not a policeman was in sight. That was during perhaps the most corrupt period in Hong Kong's history when it was the rare policeman who was not on the take.

Still swearing at the old man crouching on the ground, one of the young toughs brought back his leg in preparation for a vicious kick to the head. From out of nowhere, Duncan appeared before the hawker. Turning to face him, the hawker threw a punch with his right fist. Duncan slapped it aside with a right *guan sau* (捆手).

Then, *turning his horse*, he *covered* his right side with a right *lop sau* (擸手) and simultaneously slapped his left palm on the right side of the villain's neck, sending him tumbling to the ground. The hawker landed on some of the burning charcoals that had spilled from the small stove on which he roasted dried squids. He was too busy smothering incipient flames on his trousers to fight any more.

The moment the first hawker landed on the ground, his companion attacked from behind. Now *turning the horse* to the left, facing him, Duncan *covered* a left punch with his left forearm, simultaneously punching his opponent's nose with his right fist. As his now bleeding enemy wobbled, Duncan followed up with the *Wing Chun chase*, kicking him to the ground. Both hawkers fled the scene in panic.

Duncan helped the old man up and asked him what had happened.

"Thank you, young man. Somebody pushed me from behind and I accidentally knocked over some roasted squids. They just attacked me. They probably took advantage of my old age. You have guts. Please give me your name and tell me where you work." He was grateful.

"That's all right. I am an insurance underwriter at Sun Life of Canada. The company is in the Gloucester Building in Central."

A few weeks later, while sitting behind his desk, Duncan noticed an elderly gentleman beckoning him through the glass partition outside the office. For a brief moment he could not place the visitor, who reminded him of the incident and handed Duncan two boxes of dripping ice cream.

"Young man, thank you once again for your help. You are brave and righteous. There is something I want to teach you. I think you are the right person to receive it."

"That's not necessary."

"I am going to teach you some deadly fighting techniques."

"You're kidding!" Duncan was perplexed. His visitor must surely be joking. After all, he was helpless on the ground against those hawkers, and he was going to teach Duncan fighting techniques!

"You have doubts?"

"I am surprised, really surprised, because if you know these techniques, why didn't you defend yourself in the first place?"

"These techniques that I am going to impart to you are not for fighting at a distance. These techniques are for close combat only. But once you have your opponent in your grasp, or he grabs you, there is no way he can get away. He is as dead as a caught fish."

Duncan was, at any rate, intrigued. There would be no harm in seeing whether the old man knew what he was talking about. It was lunchtime and there were few people in the office. Duncan invited him to the coffee room. The old man stood behind him and poked a single finger into a point on Duncan's back.

"Try your best to get away from me."

No matter how hard he tried, there was no way he could escape!

"Once you are in my range, you are dead."

The old man showed an amazed Duncan several more techniques using vital points on the body. He was absolutely right. It was deadly stuff! He had never seen anything like it. In the future, these simple techniques would prove invaluable, as well as giving Duncan the confidence that he could finish off his opponents once they were within his grasp.

Over the next few weeks, the old man taught Duncan at the home of Tang Di-sheng (唐滌生), the great Cantonese opera composer. At the time, Duncan was training to become a jockey. Every morning he would drive to the Royal Hong Kong Jockey Club in the New Territories for lessons. Since his home was on Hong Kong Island and the harbour ferries did not start service early enough, he rented the ground floor of Tang's house in Kowloon Tong. It took Duncan only a few days to learn all the techniques. The rest of the time was spent practicing with the old man.

In parting, the old man admonished Duncan that the techniques were only to be taught to people on the side of good. Accordingly, he has confined the teaching of the old man's techniques to the U.S. Navy SEAL Teams Two and Four, the FBI, the Virginia Police SWAT Team and other law enforcement agencies in the United States and overseas. He never saw nor heard from the mysterious old man again.

When asked if he had not been afraid that the hawkers might have sought help from fellow gang members, Duncan replied:

It is just like *Kung Fu*. If you have to think, you are always too late to react. If I had to think then, logic would have told me not to get involved. But my gut feeling told me that I had to go. It was spontaneous. When it was over and I looked around and saw nobody coming, me and my friend went into the theatre and watched the movie.

Guts means will and courage. You need both. You need courage to apply your will and you need will to activate your courage. It is confidence, really. If you have confidence, you will have guts. Would you jump into deep water to save a drowning person if you didn't even know how to swim? If you don't know *Kung Fu*, how can you have the confidence to fight against a much bigger and stronger adversary? Once you have confidence in your own ability, you can and will fight when the time comes.

Mind you, this type of courage is nothing compared to someone who, not knowing how to swim, plunges into deep water to save a drowning person, or who, not caring for their own safety, rushes into a burning house to save another person. These are the people we call heroes. They've got real guts.

"Duncan, what is *cover*?"

冚位 (*kum wai*) or 蓋位 (*gai wai*) is a Cantonese term. The Chinese character 冚 (*kum*) does not exist in Putonghua, the official Chinese language. 蓋 (*gai*) is the equivalent which means *cover* in both Cantonese and Putonghua.

Cover is unique in *Wing Chun*. In *Wing Chun* we do not block; we *cover*. It is both a technique and a strategy. Because it does not exist in any other martial art or *Kung Fu*, it is the major difference separating *Wing Chun* from the others. Every *Wing Chun* practitioner should know how to *cover*. Without learning this, you cannot protect yourself. *Cover* is the cornerstone of *Applied Wing Chun*. It is a defensive move which enables you to be a fraction of a second ahead of your opponent. It is anticipation, both in defense and in offense.

When you see an offensive move coming at you, and you respond, it is blocking. But when you sense or anticipate an offensive move on the part of your opponent, and you initiate a defense even before it begins, it is *covering*. To see and to respond is slower than to anticipate and to initiate.

In defense, you can actually see your opponent's advance. Try to visualize this sequence. For example, if he throws a right straight punch at you, he is more likely to follow up with a left punch, because you are expected to block the first punch and expose your right side for his second punch. Instead of blocking, you *cover* your left side with any *Applied Wing Chun* techniques, snapping, slapping or rotating with your bridge arms. Immediately after the first contact, you shift your *horse* forward and *cover* the anticipated exposed right side before his left punch can even reach you. Whether he is feinting or not with his left punch, you *cover* that area anyway. By the time his left punch reaches you, your bridge arm or arms are already there, waiting comfortably for him. Meantime, you are not idle. Immediately after the second contact, one of your fists is already on its way to your opponent's exposed areas, which become targets at your mercy.

Simultaneous defense and counter-attacking is another *Wing Chun* specialty; we simply call it *cover and attack*. You always cover first. Your priority is to protect yourself in advance, whether in defense or in offense.

Self-defense is a birthright. To learn martial arts or *Kung Fu* is to exercise that right. Instructors of any martial arts systems or *Kung Fu* styles should be able to teach you how to protect yourself. Those with little fighting experience cannot teach this.

As a strategy, you deliberately leave an area *uncovered* in order to lure your opponent into a trap. Once he swallows the bait, not only will he leave exposed areas for you to attack, he will also experience, to his regret, *Wing Chun*'s simultaneous *cover and counter-attack*.

The hawker punched Duncan Leung

Leung's *guan sau* covered...

...he slapped the right side of his neck...

...and sent him tumbling to the ground

Chapter 5

THE DRAGON HEAD

Taipei
1968

A lone swordsman presents himself at Lu Su's feast
單刀赴會
(*dan dao fu hui*)
Romance of the Three Kingdoms (三國演義)
Luo Guan-zhong (羅貫中, between 1300-1400)

Luo Guan-zhong, Ming Dynasty novelist, was the author of *Romance of the Three Kingdoms* (三國演義, *san guo yan yi*), which was based on the warring for supremacy among the three kingdoms, Wei (魏, 220-265), Shu (蜀, 221-263) and Wu (吳, 222-280) during the Three Kingdoms Period (220-265), after the fall of the Han Dynasty. It is one of the four classical Chinese novels. The other three are *Water Margin* (水滸傳, *shui hu zhuan*), *Journey to the West* (西遊記, *xi you ji*) and *Dream of the Red Chamber* (紅樓夢, *hong lou meng*).

單刀赴會 (*dan dao fu hui*) was an epic about Lord Guan (關公, Guan Gong) who was invited to attend a feast given by Lu Su (魯叔) in the Kingdom of Wu, where he traveled with a small retinue. Although there was a plot to hold him hostage for the return of Jingzhou (荊州) City, he used his oratorical skills to extricate himself and returned home unscathed. It was considered a feat of bravery.

Lord Guan, sworn brother of King Liu (劉備, 161-223) and one of the Five Tiger Generals (五虎將 *wu hu jiang*) of the Shu Kingdom, was a legend renowned for his *yi qi*, courage, and high pain threshold.

It has been said that there is nothing new under the sun. Perhaps you can see Lord Guan's story reflected in the following anecdote.

"**D**uncan, there is a call for you, long distance from Taipei," a colleague of his was yelling across the office.

"Hello."

"Duncan, this is Stephen. I need your help." The voice on the other end of the telephone sounded desperate.

"Stephen, where are you?"

"I am in Taipei. I need you to come over right now."

"What is it?"

"I can't talk now. Please just come!"

Duncan took the first available flight and touched down in Taipei a few hours later. He took a taxi to Stephen's office.

Outside the door to the general office stood two heavy-set men with tattoos. One of them held a samurai sword in a sheath. They stopped Duncan and checked his identification before permitting him to enter. This seemed great fun because he thought they were shooting a movie.

Two more guards, each holding a baseball bat, stood outside Stephen's private office. Approaching the door, Duncan saw Stephen sitting behind his desk, pale and trembling. Something was very wrong.

"What's going on?"

"The boss of these guys will not let me out of here until I pay them."

"You owe them money?"

"No, I don't owe them anything. Someone else does."

"Where is he?"

"He has left the country."

It seemed that Duncan's friend had written a series of cheques to a con artist who had sold them at a discount to the wrong people. The background was that Stephen, having received a large order for ladies' shoes, had given a local Taiwanese supplier a 30% down payment for the purchase of raw materials to manufacture, the balance being due on delivery. On the date when the first assignment was due for delivery, the supplier came up empty. Stephen was furious, but was in a bind on the order. The supplier had no money to refund the down payment, and it was too late to find another factory anyway.

To solve the dilemma, Stephen paid the balance of 70% – US$400,000. However, he paid in postdated cheques, which could not legitimately be cashed. They worked out another delivery date and Stephen prayed it would work out. Close to the new date for delivery, there were rumors that the guy had left the country. Stephen went to the bank and stopped payment on the postdated cheques. For extra safety, he withdrew his money from the account and deposited it in another account to prove that he did have money in the bank before he wrote those postdated cheques.

The supplier was smarter. He sold the postdated cheques on the black market at a discount and skipped the country with the proceeds. When the buyer could not cash the cheques, they naturally went to the issuer – Stephen – to collect.

"Stephen, how can you sell postdated cheques?"

"Duncan, in Taiwan you can sell anything."

The underworld had their own ways of collecting debts. Since they were usually paid a flat fee of 25% of the amount collected, the incentive was to squeeze as much as possible out of the victim. What did they care who was right and who was wrong? That had nothing to do with business.

Duncan rose from the chair opposite Stephen, turned around and walked to the two toughs with baseball bats. They were blocking the door, preventing him from leaving the room. Duncan engaged them in light banter. He was smiling and joking, putting them at ease.

Suddenly, without warning, he grabbed a nearby stool and, lightning-quick, pinned one of the guards against the wall, one of the legs placed directly over his heart. When the other came charging, Duncan hissed between clenched teeth: "Don't come or I will kill him." The gangsters could sense the confidence he exuded. Stunned, they stopped outside the door and stood there without uttering a word. Why should they take chances unnecessarily? Also, during that period – the 1960s – foreigners in Taiwan had special privileges. They were protected like an endangered species. Punishment for crimes against them was more severe.

"I don't talk to you. Call your *elder brother* (boss) right now," Duncan demanded.

The call was made. The telephone was handed to Duncan. The voice on the other end of the line was soft and polite – entirely disarming. He knew he was speaking to the boss, the top man.

"Who is this?" Duncan asked.

The soft voice answered: "I am just like you. I am trying to help my friend."

"With swords and baseball bats?"

"People have to know that we are in business and we mean business. Why don't you and I meet and see if we can work things out."

"That is fine with me."

"How many of you?"

"Just myself with Stephen."

As a big boss would, the soft voice named the time and place, a restaurant, and they were allowed to leave.

At the appointed time, Duncan and Stephen arrived at the restaurant. They were recognized the moment they stepped out of the taxi. A young and very beautiful receptionist escorted them courteously. She led them to a set of heavy double doors guarded by two well-dressed men. As the doors were drawn open, their eyes fell upon a scene right out of a Chinese gangster film.

In the middle of a huge room was a large round table covered with a starched white tablecloth. Sitting at the far end of the table was a gentle looking man in his fifties. He was wearing a traditional Chinese outfit. Fanned out in a semicircle behind him stood at least 30 men of different heights and sizes.

Stephen was shaking. Duncan remained calm and unperturbed. The boss gestured for the pair to take the seats directly opposite him. He did not get up to greet them. Tea was poured.

Raising his teacup in greeting, he said: "*Yam cha* (drink tea)."

"*Yam cha*," replied Duncan, raising his cup.

"Since you come to negotiate on behalf of your friend, what is your offer?"

"My friend is innocent."

"It is none of my business whether he is innocent or not. If he is innocent, ask the responsible party to come and clarify. It does not matter to me as long as someone assumes the responsibility."

Before going to the meeting, Stephen and Duncan had discussed the situation. Stephen had written the cheques, and unless he could find the supplier who had fled – and that was out of the question – Stephen would have to pay. It was simply a matter of how much. A settlement would have to be negotiated.

Duncan decided to be bold: "I believe you are a reasonable man. Even if my friend were in partnership, he should be responsible for his half only."

"That is reasonable. We will accept half. That is US$200,000."

"Good. For your negotiation you will take 25%. I expect the same for my negotiation. 25% should be deducted. $150,000 is reasonable," replied Duncan, saving Stephen additional money.

"That makes sense. Settled."

In the taxi after leaving the restaurant, Stephen turned to his friend in astonishment and asked: "Duncan, do you know who you just met?"

"I have no idea who he is, but he seemed like a nice man."

"That was H.C., the dragon head of a Hong Kong triad."

Lord Guan was also well known for his incredibly high pain threshold. There is a story about him reading a book while Hua Tuo (華佗), the legendary Chinese physician and surgeon, used a knife to scrape poisoned bone from his humerus – the bone between the shoulder and the elbow.

There was a dentist in Virginia Beach, USA, who had a patient with a phobia of needles. One time, the dentist was obliged to use a scalpel to scrape infected tissue from the gums of the patient who refused local anaesthesia because of his aversion to needles. The procedure without Novocaine was so gruesome that the dental assistant refused to assist.

"Duncan, was it painful?"

"Excruciating."

"Did you scream?"

"How could I, with my mouth wide open?"

千 里 駒
(*Qian Li Ju*)

PRODIGY

Bright and shining when small may not excel when tall
小 時 了 了 大 未 必 佳
(*xiao shi liao liao, da wei bi jia*)
Kong Rong (孔融, 153-208)

Prodigies are endowed with great natural talent in one or more areas. These can be physical, artistic or intellectual, and typically manifest at an early age. Prodigy though he undoubtedly is, Duncan Leung does not believe natural ability is essential to become a skilled fighter.

He identifies the following criteria for the individual who wishes to seriously pursue a martial arts career:

• The willingness to devote the necessary time to learning (Duncan studied intensively with Yip Man and practiced for six to eight hours a day, practically every day, for four years);

• The freedom from social constraints, including familial and other relationships that would inhibit an aspirant's ability from devoting himself to learning;

• The stamina and courage to endure pain and perform the hard work necessary to achieve mastery;

• The good fortune to find a qualified instructor (such individuals are rare);

• The financial ability to pay a qualified instructor. This last is not to be overlooked. Duncan was only able to receive what he did from Yip Man because he could afford private lessons. While he himself has never been concerned about deriving a livelihood from the teaching of *Wing Chun*, for Yip Man it was his sole means of support.

Added to the above factors, innate talent is certainly helpful, but Duncan considers it secondary in importance. The foregoing obviously represents a strong and all-consuming commitment on the part of the aspirant. In this day and age, it is an unlikely combination. So let us turn to a different era, and to one who happened to be born with the inherent aptitude.

"I was very naughty when I was a small boy," Duncan says. "I could not sit still, it was as if my buttocks were pointed. I was cautioned, reprimanded and punished, physically of course. I was hyperactive. If you think corporal punishment can deter a hyperactive kid, I'm proof that this is not the case."

"How would you control such a child?"

"I would let him have more meaningful physical activities to expend his energy. Instead, my parents sent me to schools and passed their responsibility to the teachers, hoping that they could teach me how to behave."

"Did it work?"

"My parents got some peace at home when I was at school, and even more when they sent me away to a boarding school. But the teachers had a handful when they tried to instill discipline into me."

"What did they do?"

"They gave me more punishment. They tried to scare me and gave me more corporal punishment. But it didn't work on me. For some reason, I was not afraid of pain and I was not scared of anything. On the contrary, I gradually developed a sense of injustice and I sought revenge. I became a mischief-maker."

Duncan Leung was a rascal – hyperactive, mischievous, without fear. He was born and raised in a Hong Kong which no longer exists, a city in which street brawling and *Kung Fu* studio challenges were tolerated. It was a time when great *Kung Fu* artists had fled Communist China, and were forced to earn a living sharing their knowledge. More prosaically, Duncan was born into a well-to-do family which could afford Yip Man's exorbitant tuition fees.

In order for Duncan to fulfill his *yuan* (緣 destiny) to become a great martial artist, he required a *Bo Le* (a legendary connoisseur of horses – see Chapter 10). This was Yip Man, who he encountered at the right time (天時 *tian shi*) and in the right place (地利 *di li*) and with whom he established the right relationship (人和 *ren he*), even if it was predicated upon payment.

Chapter 6

YIP MAN'S FORMAL DISCIPLE

Hong Kong
1956

My life, real or unreal, who knows
一生真偽復誰知
(*yi sheng zhen wei fu shui zhi*)
Bai Ju-yi (白居易, 772-846)

Bai Ju-yi, the great poet of the Tang Dynasty (618-907), used a particular old woman to review his writing before he released it to the public. He would rewrite his work until it was completely clear to her. This famous verse describes two counselors, whose loyalty to their respective emperors, real or unreal, was only known for certain after their death.

To differentiate the real from the unreal, truth from falsehood, is not easy. To ascertain whether a *Kung Fu* artist's fighting ability or *Wugong* is real or unreal is a task fraught with difficulty. Yet, if one follows Buddha's wisdom – *Application is the only way to verify the truth* – it is possible to discern the reality behind the façade.

Although Yip Man had multitudes of students, and students of his students, throughout the world, the number of private disciples he accepted could be counted on the fingers of one hand. To these few who pledged their fidelity in the ritual of *three kneels nine kowtows* in the traditional *Sifu Worship Ceremony* he taught *Wing Chun Wugong*. This includes *Wing Chun Kung Fu* plus *Gongli*, the art of exerting power, plus the practical application of *Wing Chun* fighting techniques. Duncan Leung is the only disciple Yip Man taught personally and privately at the student's home over a period of more than four years.

Sifu Worship Ceremony

The *Sifu* relationship in *Kung Fu* is a serious business. The hierarchy of importance is Heaven (天 *tian*), earth (地 *di*), emperor (君 *jun*), parents (親 *qin*) and teacher (師 *shi*), in that order. If someone accepts you to be his disciple, it means he will be your father and mentor in *Kung Fu* forever. You respect him as if he were your natural father. As far as *Kung Fu* is concerned, you are prohibited from learning from anybody else without his permission.

Three kneels nine kowtows is part of the traditional *Sifu worship ceremony* in which the student becomes a disciple and the instructor becomes his *Sifu*. As the saying goes:

A day of *Sifu*, a lifetime of fatherhood
一日為師 終生為父
(*yi ri wei shi zhong sheng wei fu*)

Duncan Leung, one of a handful of Yip Man's private disciples, gives an account of his own *Sifu Worship Ceremony*:

"In 1955, when I was thirteen, *Sifu* accepted me to become one of his private students. A year later I became his formal disciple in a traditional *Sifu Worship Ceremony*.

"You are supposed to write on a piece of red paper, called the *bai shi tie* (拜師帖), begging the teacher to accept you as his disciple. As a teenager, I had no idea what to write, so *Sifu* taught me the words.

"I don't remember the exact wording but the content was something like this: *I swear that once I become your disciple I will never become anybody else's disciple and that I will look after you as long as you live.*

"The ceremony was performed in front of witnesses invited by *Sifu*. With both hands I gave *Sifu* the *bai shi tie,* begging him to accept me as his disciple. He accepted it and signaled the ceremony to begin.

"First was *heaven worship* (拜天 *bai tian*). With lit joss sticks clasped between my hands in front of me, I bowed respectfully three times in front of an altar placed before an open window, and then planted them into the pewter urn on the altar. Besides the pewter urn, on top of the altar was a row of small cups filled with rice wine, and a plate with a large piece of roast pork and some tangerines. The meat and fruit indicate having the same taste and flavor (分甘同味 *fen gan tong wei*), which symbolizes admittance to the family.

"Normally, *earth worship* (拜地 *bai di*) would come next. One would bow in front of a tablet, placed against the foot of a wall, on which is inscribed the Chinese characters 土地公 (*tu di gong,* earth grandfather), and then plant the joss sticks in the same urn.

"Third would be *ancestor worship* (拜祖先 *bai zu xian*). Again, one would bow in front of a set of tablets hung on the wall, on which are inscribed the names of our *Kung Fu* ancestors, and then plant the joss sticks.

"The ceremony was staged at my home. Since there were no tablets of any kind, I was spared the second and third procedures.

"The last and most important procedure is *Sifu Worship* (拜師 *bai si*). I kneeled before him and kowtowed three times. I got up and repeated the process twice more, thus completing the time-honored ritual of *three kneels nine kowtows* (三跪九叩, *san gui jiu kou*).

"While remaining on my knees after the ninth kowtow, someone passed me a cup of tea with a red date in it. I handed it to *Sifu* with both hands.

"In the same manner, I handed him a red packet with money in it. After accepting the cup of tea and the red packet, he gave me a red packet in return, also with money in it. He then taught me the martial virtues he expected of his disciples. I was too young at the time to understand what they meant.

"*Sifu* then declared, 'I have accepted you to be my disciple and I am your *Sifu* now. I am of the Sixth Generation and you are of the Seventh Generation. I will teach you all the *Wing Chun Kung Fu* I know and teach you how to apply the techniques. You will have to work hard. You have two, three elder *Kung Fu* brothers, and I will introduce you to them some day.'

"I got up and the ritual was complete. From that moment onward he became my *Sifu* and I, who was already his private student, became his formal disciple."

"Duncan, I read a book in which a Mr. Yung Sing Yip (容成業) described Leung Ting as the 'Closed Door Disciple (閉門弟子)' of Yip Man. Is this true?"

"I am sure this serious mistake was unintentional. I doubt Leung Ting would ever claim that he was the disciple of Yip Man, even though *Sifu* might have taught him during his period of illness before he died."

"Do you have a copy of this book?"

"Leung Ting sent me a copy in 1984, asking for my opinion."

"Did he write anything on the book?"

"Yes, he addressed me as his *Shixu* (師叔), younger uncle in *Kung Fu*."

"So, he is a generation after you."

"Yes, he is of the Eighth Generation. The phrase *When drinking water, remember its source* (飲水思源 *yin shui si yuan*) means *'Don't ever forget from whom you have learned your skills.'* Your *Sifu*, no matter how mediocre, is your *Kung Fu* father for life once you become his disciple. To call your *Kung Fu* grandfather your *Kung Fu* father is ridiculous. If this were to occur, it would mean you have moved one generation upward, and your *Kung Fu* father would be demoted in relation to you to become your *Kung Fu* brother!

"How could any disciple show such disrespect to his father in *Kung Fu*? This would upset the natural relationships. I do not believe *Sifu* could have done something ridiculous like that to upset the order of succession. He did not have to be the disciple of Liang Bi (梁璧), son of Liang Zan (梁贊), to learn from him."

"Duncan, do you think Professor Leung Ting should correct Mr. Yung's mistake as a token of respect for his *Sifu*, Leung Sheung (梁相), and the *Wing Chun* clan?"

"That is entirely up to him. It is no business of mine."

"Duncan, tell me, what did your *Sifu* mean when he said you had two, three elder *Kung Fu* brothers?"

"*Sifu* meant that he had accepted only two, three disciples before me. They all went through the same ritual."

"What are you talking about? I thought some of your elder *Kung Fu* brothers were his disciples."

"No, none of the elder brothers I knew at the time were his disciples. They were his students."

"I am confused. Have you met those two, three elder brothers?"

"No, I never met them."

"Do you know who they are?"

"No, *Sifu* never told me who they were."

"How many formal disciples did your *Sifu* have?"

"As far as I know, only a handful."

"You mean the rest were all students."

"Yes, as far as I know."

"Did they all learn how to apply *Wing Chun*?"

"I don't know for sure."

"How about students – did they learn how to apply *Wing Chun* from *Sifu*?"

"They could have done."

Renegade Disciple

"Duncan, just as a matter of interest, have you ever expelled any of your formal disciples?"

"Yes, once. It was back in 1975, when I was still in New York City."

"What happened?"

"I found out that he was working as a pimp for the triads, and I tried to persuade him to change his job and leave the secret society."

"Did he?"

"He said it was his private business. So I asked him to leave."

"Is he teaching *Wing Chun*?"

"I think so. I heard that he denied learning *Wing Chun* from me and declared he learned from another of my elder *Kung Fu* brothers, who happened to have passed away when he was still a child."

"Who was the guy you expelled?"

"He was my ex-disciple J. L."

Chapter 7

I FIGHT FOR MY LIFE

Macau
1949

Illness reaches the incurable spot
病入膏肓
(*bing ru gao huang*)
Han Fei-zi (韓非子, 280-233 B.C.)

Han Fei-zi was a philosopher during the Warring States Period (475-221 B.C.). His book of 100,000 words, based on Confucian, Taoist, Legalist and other schools of thought, is named after him. It contains familiar fables and proverbs which have made it one of the most popular books for centuries. Unfortunately, Han Fei-zi had a speech impediment, which did not endear him to the rulers of his time. He was imprisoned and poisoned in confinement.

病入膏肓 (*bing ru gao huang*) comes from one of his many proverbs. It warns that a ruler should actively remedy a social or political problem – as if it were an illness of the body – at an early stage before it becomes an incurable condition.

諱疾忌醫 (*hui ji ji yi*) is an idiom to describe an individual who hides his illness to avoid unpleasant treatment. Delaying diagnosis and treatment allows the illness to progress to the stage where it is irreversible.

In December 1941, the Imperial Japanese army invaded and captured Hong Kong. Duncan Leung was born in that occupied city six months later, in June 1942. Because of food shortages, most families were allowed to leave Hong Kong if they had the means, and his family moved to the nearby Macau when Duncan was a year old. They would live there for over a decade, moving back to Hong Kong when Duncan was thirteen in 1955.

Now a Special Administrative Region, Macau was a Portuguese colony until December 1999, when it was returned to China. It is a peninsula on the west bank of the Pearl River, about an hour's ride by hovercraft from Hong Kong. Macau is a renowned pleasure spot, famous – and infamous – for its casinos and entertainments of every description.

The family businesses included wholesaling fish and poultry, and newspaper publication, both in Hong Kong and Macau.

Duncan's father had four wives, which was both legal and common among the privileged classes in those days. As the eldest of the two sons of the fourth and youngest wife, Duncan was loved and spoiled.

Duncan relates:

I was seven when I became seriously ill. At first, it wasn't a serious condition. One of my premolars was extracted from the lower right side of my mouth. But the gum became infected, probably due to contaminated instruments. All that was needed was to lance the boil and drain the infection.

However, my parents did not trust Western-trained doctors because they didn't believe in operations, even minor ones. They preferred traditional Chinese healers, who seemed to know all about your illnesses and diagnoses by simply feeling your pulse.

There was no need to go through blood tests, X-rays or other investigations. Once a diagnosis was made, herbal medicine was prescribed and occasionally acupuncture administered. In my case, the diagnosis was 'too much fire element'.

The treatment was supposed to cure my illness and achieve equilibrium in my body. But it looked as though I had to get worse before I could get better. The swelling was getting bigger and my temperature was rising. My parents were getting worried, and they had no alternative but to send me to 白馬行 (*bai ma hang* – literally, White Horse Company), a private Western hospital on Rue Pedro Nolasco Da Silva. The hospital is no longer there. They could not accept the suggestion of an operation on their son. It would be too dangerous.

They didn't realize the danger was not from a scalpel or an operation, but from the bacteria causing the infection. I received injection after injection of antibiotics. My rear end was jabbed so many times, a painful experience I would never forget. As a result, I developed a phobia of needles. Many years later, in Sydney, Australia, a dentist was horrified when I told him to extract my rotten molar without local anesthesia. I could feel his hands shaking while operating. He should have taken a tranquilizer. He was more afraid than I was.

In any event, my condition continued to deteriorate. The infection spread up my right cheek into my jaw and lymph nodes. The right side of my face swelled like a pumpkin. The doctor told my parents that unless they allowed him to operate, I would die of septicemia. At this point, they had no choice. I was under the knife, and the operation lasted for hours. The surgeon had to chip off rotten bone from my jaw, but the operation was successful. Finally, my temperature subsided and I got better slowly, very slowly. But it left me with an indented scar below my right cheek, which remains to this day. I was in hospital for over nine months!

As a result of missing so much school, I was way behind the other kids. However, my mother would not allow me to repeat a year, because to do so would have cost the family 'face'. While staying back and repeating school would have certainly given me a better educational foundation, I was continuously promoted, no doubt as a result of my parents' generous donations to schools I attended. Thus, according to the Chinese way, we 'save face'.

I had been ashamed to reveal the number of schools I had attended to anyone until the day I learned, to my amazement, that one of my partners had attended ten schools, all in Hong Kong, doubling my number! With a double digit like that, you would have thought this guy must be a failure as far as education is concerned. I am happy to tell you that he was admitted to a prestigious medical school in London and became a qualified medical practitioner within the shortest time possible. He did repeat one year in a secondary school. *Good foundation is important in everything. Forget 'face'.*

My parents decided I should practice more sports to strengthen my body, and *Kung Fu* was one of them. They arranged for several *Kung Fu* instructors to teach me. I was quick to pick up whatever they taught me and I was keen to practice.

I felt as though I was born to practice *Kung Fu*.

Observation (望 *wang*), auscultation and olfaction (聞 *wen*), enquiry (問 *wen*), and pulse feeling and palpation (切 *qie*) are the *Four Methods of Diagnosis* (四診 *si zhen*) in traditional Chinese medicine. Pulse feeling has been dramatized and mystified.

By simply feeling a patient's pulses from the wrists, a skillful practitioner of traditional Chinese medicine can render an informed diagnosis. To treat a common person, a healer puts his fingers to the patient's wrists and feels the various pulses. In former times, to treat a female member of the royal family, a royal physician was only allowed to feel the pulses indirectly from a thread tied to either royal wrist!

Before the introduction of Western medical knowledge to China, traditional Chinese medicine was the only treatment available to the people. Skepticism of Western medicine was due to ignorance and superstition. It was available only to the educated and the wealthy class – and they would try it only as a last resort.

Today, China has achieved a harmonious blend of traditional Chinese medicine, based upon centuries of empirical observation and trial and error, together with Western medicine, supported by scientific research, technology and laboratory investigation.

Chapter 8

First Street Fight

Macau
1954

Newborn calves are unafraid of tigers
初 生 之 犢 不 怕 虎
(*chu sheng zhi du bu pa hu*)
Romance of The Three Kingdoms (三國演義)
Luo Guan-zhong (羅貫中)

Newborn calves are unafraid of tigers (初生之犢不怕虎) refers to people too young to know what fear is. When you are born, you fear nothing. This idiom is a compliment to young people who are often brave and dare to try anything, even though they may be naïve.

Fear is mostly acquired. If you ask a toddler to jump off a staircase, he will if you promise you will catch him. If you don't, he will learn from the falling experience not to jump from the staircase again and not to trust you. You learn fear from your own experience, painful or fearful, or from experiences related to you by others. As you grow older you learn there is a lot more to fear. At the same time you also learn from experience to overcome fears acquired earlier in life. You learn to acquire fear and you also learn to overcome fear.

For several centuries Macau was a Portuguese colony, and the descendants of the Portuguese colonists enjoyed special privileges. They typically mastered three languages – Portuguese, English and Cantonese. Most of them worked for the Government or had relatives in charge of Government departments. They felt they were superior to the native Chinese and they behaved in that manner.

One day, the 12-year-old Duncan was riding his bicycle along Francisco Xavier Pereira Street (啤利啦街) close to the pavement. A group of five or six Portuguese teenagers were loitering and talking a few meters ahead of his path. Just as he was about to pass them, one of the bigger ones – maybe 18 years old – kicked the rear wheel, causing him to fall hard onto the ground. The rest of the teenagers laughed.

Furious, Duncan picked himself off the ground and tackled the one who had kicked him. Even though he went down because Duncan's attack was totally unexpected, the Portuguese – twice the size of his Chinese victim – was soon on top, repeatedly punching Duncan. The rest of them gathered around and kicked Duncan, insulting him, while their friend pinned him from above with his weight and slugged him.

Finally, they let Duncan go and walked away. Duncan hobbled to his feet, retrieved his bicycle, and limped away.

This was a lesson Duncan would never forget. He realized he needed not only to learn better *Kung Fu*, but also actual fighting experience. As Duncan would later repeatedly tell his students: "Learning and practicing *Kung Fu* without actual fighting is like learning to swim on dry land. You may know all the strokes, but you cannot learn to swim until you get into deep water."

As he pedalled away from the scene of his humiliation, his face swollen, eyes blackened, stomach painful from the weight of the Portuguese youth, tears were in his eyes, but Duncan did not cry. He did not forget either.

Many years went by. In 1964, exactly ten years later, shortly after his return from Australia, Duncan and a friend decided to visit Macau. Walking through the neighborhood where he had been assaulted, he saw the same youth who had beaten him years before. The Portuguese had hardly changed over the decade that had passed. Duncan stood before his tormentor and asked if he knew who he was. He didn't, but the incident was seared in Duncan's memory.

Duncan asked if he didn't live on such and such street. "Yeah, that's my block," the Portuguese replied.

Duncan then refreshed his recollection of what he had done to a child half his size, and gave him a shove. The Portuguese said he didn't remember. Duncan shoved him again, aiming to provoke him. It worked: the Portuguese got angry, took a swing at Duncan, and the fight was on. His pent-up rage boiling to the surface, Duncan smashed his elbow into the Portuguese's ribs, breaking a few and sending him rolling onto the ground. Grabbing his head by the hair, Duncan rubbed his face back and forth over the cobblestones, saying: "Now you'll remember. Every time you see your face in the mirror, you will remember!"

Confidence is an acquired trait. You are not born with it, nor can you inherit it. From the very moment you are born, you need protection to survive. Under the umbrella of your parents, you learn confidence in walking, speaking, meeting people. You are constantly taught, reminded and sometimes punished for misbehavior and mistakes. You learn from education and later from experience to believe in your own abilities and in yourself.

Learning to ride a bicycle is a good example. You are worried that you might fall off the bike and hurt yourself. Do your parents discourage you from trying to learn? Of course not. They realize it's a necessary part of your growth, even thought you might – probably will – fall off at first and scrape yourself. In the beginning, you grip the handlebar very tightly because you are afraid of falling off. Once you master balance, you begin to relax and loosen your grip because you have gained confidence in yourself, and you know you will not fall. As you become more skillful, you may let go of one hand first and then both hands to show off. Your confidence has enabled you to walk tall with pride in this new skill, whatever your size or shape. Learning *Kung Fu* is no different.

Self-defense is a birthright. Without knowledge of self-defense, children are more likely to be bullied or beaten. Parents should encourage their children to learn to protect themselves, exercising a basic right. *Applied Wing Chun* is a system especially designed for the weak.

To learn *Kung Fu* is to learn how to defend not just yourself but also others. Being able to protect yourself is the first step to gain self-confidence. Self-confidence helps you overcome fear. The conquering of fear leads to self-esteem.

Chapter 9

Bruce Lee And I

Hong Kong
1955–1958

Hidden dragons, crouching tigers
藏 龍 臥 虎
(*cang long wo hu*)
Ji Gong Quan Zhuan (濟公全傳)
Guo Xiao-ting (郭小亭)

Ji Gong Quan Zhuan (濟公全傳) is a popular Chinese novel written by Guo Xiao-ting during the Qing Dynasty (1644-1911). It was about an unorthodox Buddhist monk called Ji Dian (濟顛) who lived in the Song Dynasty (960-1279) and was later deified.

藏龍臥虎 (*cang long wo hu*) is a description of true masters who remain inconspicuous. They maintain a low profile and are hard to find. Unlike frogs in the well, when they roar the world listens and when they move the earth trembles.

As Duncan tells it:

I had an older cousin, Zi Luo-lian (紫羅蓮) who was a well-known film actress. She was quite popular and was known on screen as the perennial suffering victim, a part she played to perfection. All her films were sad. I cannot remember a movie in which she did not cry. She is alive and well and she has been a pious Christian for many years.

I met Bruce Lee through Lou-lian who was acquainted with Bruce's father, an actor by the name of Li Hai-quan (李海泉). Bruce was about two and a half years older than I was and we had known each other since we were small. He was a child actor, and everyone called him by his stage name, Li Xiao-long (李小龍) – *Lee the little dragon.* Bruce and I would see each other several times a year at gatherings.

When my family moved to Hong Kong in 1955 because my mother wanted me to go to high school there, we attended the same school and we saw each other often. A lot of our spare time was spent on the rooftop of our four-story house in North Point. Even though he was a little older than me, our personalities complemented one another and we got along really well.

Bruce Lee did not know much *Kung Fu* when I moved to Hong Kong. He learned stage fighting, including some boxing techniques. I taught him the *Kung Fu* I learned in Macau.

I was his *sifu* and I beat him every time we sparred until one day…

"Hung *chai*, I have something new to show you," Bruce was yelling from downstairs. I was at Luo-lian's home at Prat Avenue in Kowloon.

'Chai' means son or little boy. It is a Cantonese custom to call a boy 'chai' after the last character of his name. My last character is 'Hung' so they all called me 'Hung chai'.

"Come upstairs," I yelled back.

"I have learned *Wing Chun.*"

"*Wing Chun?* What is that?"

"It is a kind of *Kung Fu* invented by a lady."

"So, you are learning from a woman."

"No, I am learning from Yip Man. He is a man."

"Show me," I said.

We went to the balcony on the third floor. He attacked me first with the *chase* and *chain punches,* and busted my nose. I thought he caught me because there was not enough room for me to retreat. We went up to the rooftop and tried again. The same thing happened. He busted my mouth too. It wasn't a question of limited space because, assuming the rooftop wasn't big enough to dodge his punches, we went to King's Park on Wylie Road and the result was the same. No matter what I tried, I could not get him. It was Bruce who was doing all the damage – a first! Blood ran down my nose. My face and chest hurt, not to mention my ego. I was convinced of this *Kung Fu* invented by a woman.

"Why don't you come with me to learn *Wing Chun* from Yip Man," Bruce suggested.

I couldn't wait. Bruce brought me to *Sifu*'s studio in Sham Shui Po (深水埗), a Kowloon district adjacent to Shek Kip Mei (石硤尾), one of the most undesirable neighborhoods in Hong Kong, where *dragons and snakes jumbled together* (龍蛇混雜 *long she hun za*). It was a resettlement area for refugees from China, squatters from the streets and homeless victims of fires. It was infested with triads, drug traffickers, whores, criminals and gamblers, but there were also *hidden dragons and crouching tigers*.

Bruce introduced me to *Sifu*, telling him that I wanted to learn *Wing Chun* too.

Sifu was a diminutive man, gentle, friendly and a man of few words.

"What is your name?"

"Leung Shiu Hung."

"Have you learned *Kung Fu* before?"

"I have learned *Hung Kuen* (洪拳)."

"Show me."

I showed him what I could do.

"Not bad. Your stance is quite steady. Bring me eight dollars tomorrow and you can start."

"I have money here," I said, and handed him some bills. He was impressed that a schoolboy had eight dollars on him.

"Ah Chant, come and *open fists* (開拳 *kai quan*) with him," Yip Man called.

The first person who *opened my fists* (initiated me into learning *Wing Chun*) was Ng Chant (伍燦). *Sifu* never taught beginners. It was elder *Kung Fu* brothers, whoever was available, who taught us. So I had many instructors then.

Chapter 10

Yip Man And I

Hong Kong
1955-1959

Thousand-li horse met Bo Le
驥 遇 伯 樂
(*ji yu Bo Le*)
Zhan Guo Ce (戰國策)
Liu Xiang (劉向)

Zhan Guo Ce (戰國策), written by Liu Xiang (劉向) during the Han Dynasty (206B.C.-A.D.220), recorded the stratagems recommended by counselors to their emperors during the Warring States Period (475-221 B.C.).

Bo Le (伯樂), a connoisseur of horses during the Spring and Autumn Period (770-474 B.C.), was legendary for his uncanny ability of judging horseflesh. The story is told that one day he spotted an old nag towing a cart of salt uphill, and recognized immediately that it was a *thousand-li* horse (a 驥 *ji* which can cover 500 kilometers a day). He was desolate and in tears. To show his respect he went over to the animal and covered it with his cloak. The horse, similarly moved, neighed loudly to heaven, as if to ask why its talents had not been noticed until that day.

Only when there is a Bo Le, can there be a *thousand-li* horse

世有伯樂然後有千里馬

(*shi you Bo Le, ran hou you qian li ma*)

While *thousand-li* horses are not common, men like Bo Le are
even rarer

千里馬常有而伯樂不常有

(*qian li ma chang you, er Bo Le bu chang you*)

Han Yu (韓愈, 768-824)

Han Yu, one of the *Eight Prose Masters of the Tang-Song Period* (唐宋八大家 *Tang Song ba da jia*) during the Tang Dynasty (618-907) and the Song Dynasty (960-1279) stated that individuals with the gift of spotting extraordinary talent are the rarest of all, and without a master who can recognize talent, these qualities often go undeveloped. (It might be noted that Duncan Leung – a *thousand-li* horse – was born in the Year of the Horse.)

Yip Man was born in Foshan in 1893, during the reign of Emperor Guang Xu (光緒, 1875-1908). His family was well off, and he was raised and educated in the traditional manner.

By the time he was 13, he was accepted as the last disciple of Chen Hua-shun (陳華順), who was the most outstanding disciple of Liang Zan (梁贊). His *Sifu* was in his seventies when he was accepted, and it was Wu Zhong-su (吳仲素), his second elder *Kung Fu* brother, who undertook the responsibility of teaching him.

In 1908, when he was 15, Yip Man became a boarder at St. Stephen's College in Stanley in Hong Kong. It was his good fortune that, while in Hong Kong, he met Liang Bi (梁璧), the son of Liang Zan. By the time he returned to Foshan, he had plumbed the depths of Liang Bi's knowledge of *Wing Chun*. The superiority of Yip Man's *Wing Chun* led to speculation that secret *Kung Fu* knowledge had been passed from Liang Zan to Liang Bi to him.

Yip Man witnessed the fall of the Qing Dynasty in 1911, the birth of the Republic of China under the presidency of Sun Yat-sen (孫中山), and the Kuomintang (國民黨) regime under the leadership of Chiang Kai-shek (蔣介石). He survived the Second World War and the occupation by the Japanese Imperial Army between 1937 and 1945.

After Japan was defeated in 1945, Yip Man served as a police chief in Foshan, from which vantage point he witnessed the failure of the Kuomintang regime and its retreat to Taiwan. Before the birth of the People's Republic of China on 1 October 1949, he escaped to Hong Kong without his family to avoid an expected purge by the victorious Communists led by Mao Zedong (毛澤東).

To earn his livelihood in Hong Kong, Yip Man began teaching *Wing Chun Kung Fu*. Considering the state of Hong Kong's economy at the time and the huge number of refugees flooding across the border, establishing a school was a formidable undertaking. However, as a result of Yip Man's efforts, *Wing Chun* rapidly became recognized in Hong Kong *Kung Fu* circles as a legitimate system of martial arts.

At different times and at different places throughout his career, Yip Man had accepted students. However, it was the students he taught in the 1950s in Hong Kong who built the reputation of *Wing Chun*. Collectively they were known simply as the *Wing Chun* fighters. Among them were Duncan's *Kung Fu* elder brothers, the late Liang Xiang (梁相), Zhao Yun (招允), Ye Bo-qing (葉步青), Huang Chun-liang (黃淳樑) and Bruce Lee. Xu Shang-tian

(徐尚田) and Luo Yao (駱耀) are in Hong Kong. Zhang Xue-jian (張學健) is in the United States. William Cheung (張卓慶) is in Australia. They attracted media attention and made headlines by challenging and fighting against the various already-established *Kung Fu* schools.

Many students, Duncan Leung among them, paid Yip Man a monthly fee of eight Hong Kong dollars to learn *Wing Chun.* The *Sifu* himself never taught beginners. For months, Duncan never saw him teach anyone. It was the various elder brothers who taught novices.

In those days students started fighting against each other soon after learning *siu nim tau, chi sau,* and *chum kiu.* Senior students were constantly seeking opportunities to fight in the streets or studios of other established systems.

Duncan, together with his friend Bruce Lee, followed the seniors and witnessed many fights, including the challenge tournament at the Queen Elizabeth Stadium in Mongkok (旺角) between *White Crane* (白鶴派 *bai he pai*) and *Wing Chun* adherents.

In his words:

One such contest was between Wong Shen-leung (黃淳樑 Huang Chun-liang) representing *Wing Chun* and another young man Ni Wo-tang (倪沃棠) representing *White Crane.* It took place on a typical platform enclosed by ropes. When the whistle was blown, Huang kicked first, missing Ni. He then followed up with *chain punches,* some of which hit their mark. Ni was throwing punches at Huang even as he retreated, and some of these landed on Huang. Huang chased Ni around the ring. Blood was pouring from Ni's nose, but Huang was exhausted from chasing him. Finally the umpire stopped the fight, declaring the bout was a draw because both opponents had drawn blood and were injured.

It was an anticlimax to one of the most publicized fighting events in the colony. Spectators dispersed in disappointment. The fighting itself did not impress anybody, including me.

The press seized on the event. Claims and counterclaims were published. The contest, which was supposed to have finished in a draw, continued in the newspapers. As a result, there arose animosity between *Wing Chun* and *White Crane*, which lasted for a long time.

Unofficial tournaments between *Wing Chun* and other styles took place frequently. The results were invariably the same – there were never clear-cut winners and losers. Basically, opponents exchanged blows and kicks. Fighters usually bled and drew blood; both were in pain at the end of the match. The *Wing Chun* fighters suffered too.

After watching these tournaments, and seeing the results, I gathered my courage and went to *Sifu*.

"*Sifu*, I want to quit *Wing Chun*."

"Why?"

"It is useless."

"Be patient. In a few more years you will be a very good fighter because you have talent."

"I have watched all these fights. My *Kung Fu* elder brothers have learned and practiced all these years and they never win fights convincingly. They might win but they are hit so many times too. If this is all the *Wing Chun* you are going to teach me, I am quitting."

"Hung *chai*, you want to fight better?"

"Yes, *Sifu*."

"Do you have money?"

"Yes." I answered without hesitation.

"Can you afford three hundred dollars a month?"

"I can pay that. But why should I?"

Sifu then showed me a few things and it was as if a light bulb was switched on in my head. Suddenly, it all made sense to me, because what he demonstrated was so logical. But *Sifu* was surprised that a child could actually understand.

I had no real sense of what HK$300 represented. What did a spoiled 13-year-old child know about the value of money? In fact, three hundred Hong Kong dollars a month was a lot of money at this time, but I did not realize that until I was older. This was the era of refugees escaping from behind the Bamboo Curtain. Many of them lived in shanties up in the foothills. Beggars, drifters and squatters were numerous. Having any job at all was considered lucky. During this period, a live-in amah who cleaned, did the laundry, cooked, minded the children – you name it – was paid just HK$30 a month. A private chauffeur, driving and cleaning the automobile, was paid HK$80 a month. Even high school graduates employed by the Government were paid only HK$180 a month!

Each of Yip Man's regular students paid HK$8 a month to learn from him. I asked *Sifu* what he was going to teach me. He told me about the *collision punch* (衝門搥) – how to kick with power from the waist and stance. Most importantly, *Sifu* explained *Wing Chun* theory in a way that made so much sense that a 13-year-old boy like myself could easily understand. I was very happy when I went home.

"Mum, please give me three hundred dollars."

"What? Three hundred dollars! What for?" She was playing mahjong, always the best time to ask her for money. She didn't want to be disturbed and would do anything just to get me out of her sight as soon as possible.

"I need the money to pay for private tuition."

"That is a good idea, but why so much?"

"I have a lot to catch up on. I have found a Western lady to teach me English. "

"You want to study?" She was suspicious.

"Sure. I want to learn and improve." I was not lying, although I meant it about *Kung Fu*.

"Take the money and tell me later." A generous mother with a spoiled brat always paid on the spot.

I couldn't wait, and went back to *Sifu*'s studio the very next day. He was surprised that I was back so soon. And he was even more surprised that I came up with the money. I think he looked upon me as a gift from heaven. There couldn't be any doubt of my sincerity and determination. And for three hundred dollars a month, he would take time and have the patience to go into detail and make sure I learned.

After the ritual of *three kneels nine kowtows* I became his formal disciple and started learning *Wing Chun Kung Fu* in earnest. *Sifu* taught and constantly corrected me. We went back and forth until I figured out the best way of applying the techniques.

Over the next four years, I learned everything about how to apply *Wing Chun*. I was a quick study to begin with and I threw myself into practice, averaging six hours a day. I exhausted him, being very aggressive about acquiring his knowledge. Our relationship went beyond *Sifu* and disciple. He was like a father to me. I think I was almost like an experiment to him – a challenge, as Eliza Doolittle was to Henry Higgins. But our bond was strictly martial arts: neither of us had any interest in discussing other topics.

Sifu was a very pleasant man. He hardly ever said no to anyone who cared to ask him a question, whether related to *Kung Fu* or not. His answers, while not necessarily direct, were always positive and encouraging. Even before I began studying with him privately, I could not help but notice that different students performed the same techniques differently. Nevertheless, *Sifu* would always tell the student he was correct and to "just keep practicing." Thus, each student came to believe that the way he was practicing was the right way. When a student asked a question, his way was to respond with a question: "Well, what do you think?" no matter what the answer was, he would invariably say "Yes, you're right. Excellent!" or words to that effect. Eventually, there were contentions among the senior students as to whose moves and techniques were correct and effective, because *Sifu* had said each was right.

"*Sifu*, how come the same moves and techniques are performed differently by each of us?" I asked.

"You are too young to understand why. I will tell you when you get older."

That was the answer I got at the time!

Still, rumors circulated among senior students that Yip Man was withholding knowledge from his students to maintain his superiority. If he taught them everything, then there would be no gap between him and his students. The word was that he was protecting his livelihood. Some of *Sifu's* students had already opened *Wing Chun* studios within walking distance from his, in direct competition with him. He charged eight dollars per month, and some of his students were charging less. Competition for students was fierce. Since Yip Man was the *Sifu* of them all, those who could afford eight dollars would study at his studio. Those who could afford less went to his students. Eight Hong Kong dollars was considered a large sum of money then, when workers made fifty or sixty dollars a month.

Once I asked *Sifu*: "Did those senior students learn everything from you?" He shrugged and replied: "They are teachers already, and have their own studios. They don't need to come to me any more."

It has been said that it is not right to *cover one's evil deeds and praise good ones* (隱惡揚善 *yin e yang shan*). Even the errors of emperors and presidents eventually see the light of day.

In 1847, in the wake of its defeat in the Opium War, the weak Qing Dynasty was forced to sign the Treaty of Nanking, as a result of which China became an open market for opium imported by the European states. The Opium War also marked the beginning of the downfall of the Qing, and it was a disaster for China, which became a nation of addicts supplied by colonial powers that grew rich from the misery of its people.

Sifu was from a prominent family in Foshan, educated both there and in Hong Kong. During the period of his youth, it was common for young men from wealthy families to acquire the habit of opium smoking. It was as socially acceptable as cigarette smoking is today. *Sifu* participated in this convention.

With the overthrow of the Qing, opium smoking became illegal in Hong Kong, though it was not strictly enforced. However, opium became increasingly more expensive on the black market. When I knew *Sifu*, he was on opium, an expensive habit. He needed a dependable source of income to feed his addiction in Hong Kong and to feed his family in Foshan. Was this evil on his part? Who was to judge *Sifu*?

Chapter 11

Private Wing Chun Curriculum

Hong Kong
1955-1959

To perfect an assignment, first sharpen your tools
工 欲 善 其 事 必 先 利 其 器
(*gong yu shan qi shi, bi xian li qi qi*)
The Analects of Confucius
Confucius

Confucius (or Kongzi), the founder of Confucianism, a school of thought during the Spring and Autumn Period (770- 474 B.C.), is probably the best known of the Chinese philosophers. In *Kung Fu*, sharpening one's tools is not enough. One must learn how to apply them. Sharp tools can be dangerous in the hands of novices, and perilous to those who have not learned to use them properly.

One day, *Sifu* spoke to me very seriously: "Hung *chai*, what I am going to teach you now is not just *Wing Chun*. I am going to teach you how to really apply the system."

"What do you mean?"

"You will learn to fight. Every move you make and every technique you learn will be for fighting. If you follow everything I teach and practice hard enough you will become a great fighter."

"Yes, *Sifu*."

"Do you believe everything I say?"

"Of course."

"If you believe everything I say, you will never become a great fighter."

"Why shouldn't I believe you? You are my *Sifu*."

"Don't just believe me. Try them out for yourself. And when you have a problem, I will correct it."

Sifu taught me how to use the techniques and explained to me how they worked. The difference was obvious. I was getting personal attention, one on one.

Exercises

In *Wing Chun,* exercises are preliminary training devices designed to train the practitioner's sensitivity and enhance strength. The exercises, including *chi sau*, are not fighting techniques, a factor not always understood even by instructors.

Siu nim tau (小念頭, *xiao nian tou*)

Siu nim tau is the primary form, and it is not difficult to learn. The basic moves are simple and easy and can be learned within a few days. Thereafter, it is reasonable for the average student to practice for three months in order to become familiar with the moves and to build up necessary strength in the arms and legs. *Siu nim tau,* along with *chum kiu* and *biu tze,* is like the alphabet (or brushstrokes, as the case may be) of *Wing Chun.* It forms the foundation for practice, and is of paramount importance.

Chi sau (黐手, *zhan shou*)

As stated earlier, *chi sau* is unique in *Wing Chun.* It is a drill to improve one's sensitivity in contact with, and in control of, the opponent. The most important aspect is to train the student to *cover* exposed areas. Facing one another, two students intertwine their forearms and move in scheduled motions, with basic movements they have learned from *siu nim tau*, initially with one arm and later with both arms. *Chi sau* helps develop the sense of contact with, and awareness of the intentions of, the opponent. Initially, the average student will learn sensing in three months, but to be good at it will take much longer. Eventually, one should be able to perform *chi sau* blindfolded.

Chum kiu (尋橋, *xun qiao*)

Chum kiu also comprises basic components of *Wing Chun*, being the secondary form, which involves leg movements. Whereas in *siu nim tau*, the horse stance does not move, in *chum kiu*, by moving the horse stance one learns how to support and coordinate the arm movements, and how to exert power.

Biu tze (標指, *biao zhi*)

Biu tze is the advanced form. It is the management and application of power or, more appropriately, power penetration. It teaches one how to accumulate power at one single point, and how to extend the shoulder blades to gain further reach. The *inch punch* (長橋發力, *chang qiao fa li*) is from shoulder blade extension.

Techniques

Continuing our analogy, *siu nim tau, chum kiu,* and *biu tze* are all parts of the alphabet of *Wing Chun*. Techniques can be understood as the words and phrases. They are combinations of basic moves one derives from *siu nim tau, chum kiu,* and *biu tze*. Just as there is no limit to the number of words that can be formed from the letters of the alphabet, the number of techniques is limitless. Techniques are essential to achieve fighting proficiency.

Wooden Man (木人椿, *mu ren zhuang*)

Wooden Man is what its name implies – a mock man, a wooden dummy. There are 108 techniques involved with *Wooden Man*. *Drill Wooden Man* (上椿, *shang zhuang*) is the practice of those techniques. It is relatively easy. *Dismantle Wooden Man* (拆椿 *chai zhuang*) is the application of those techniques in fighting with the *Wooden Man*. *Chai zhuang* literally means 'breaking it down', and it is very difficult. In practice, one moves around the *Wooden Man*, which of course is static. In actual fighting, the opponent is moving. The application of techniques is therefore very different. Interestingly, according to Duncan, Yip Man declined to teach Bruce Lee *Dismantle Wooden Man* (see Chapter 19), without which, one simply cannot fight effectively with the *Wing Chun* techniques.

Eight-Chop Knives (八斬刀, *ba zhan dao*)

To manipulate the knives (see Chapter 17) is easy. To apply them in combat is both very difficult and extremely dangerous.

Tripoles (品字椿, *pin zi zhuang*)

The *Tripoles* are central to the art and prowess of kicking in *Wing Chun Kung Fu*. *Wing Chun* kicks (see Chapter 12) are most effective and most difficult to defend against because of the shortness of distance they travel. *Wing Chun* kicks land by the time an opponent sees them coming. They are called *under skirt kicks* (裙裏脚, *qun li jiao*) or *invisible kicks* (無形脚, *wu xing jiao*).

Six and A Half Point Pole (六點半棍, *lui dian ban gun*)

The long pole (see Chapter 13) was not an original part of this system of *Kung Fu*, because the female founder of *Wing Chun* found it too long and too heavy. Requiring tremendous strength, it represents a deviation from the central philosophy of *Wing Chun*.

"Duncan, are you good with the pole?"

"No, nowhere near to what *Sifu* could do."

"Have you fought with it?"

"No, how am I going to carry it around with me? I am not the Monkey King."

"Duncan, did Yip Man teach you how to fight with the knives?"

"Yes, he said I was the best with knives."

"Have you ever actually fought with them?"

"I must admit I have."

When I became *Sifu*'s private student, we started from scratch and returned to the basics. It was a completely different ball game altogether. Each move in *siu nim tau* alone had its own meaning and application. It was explained to me in great detail. I had to visualize an opponent in front of me and imagine how to apply the moves (*siu nim tau* means 'little imagination'). I practiced each move repeatedly until it became part of me. I enjoyed the repetition because I understood why. *Straight line*, *center line* and *power application* were all very simple and logical once they were explained properly.

Chi sau with *Sifu* personally was like a *pas de deux* in ballet. He led and I followed, and when he passed the lead to me he pushed and pulled me along. Gradually he changed the pace and shifted the power and I learned to change with him accordingly. Anybody with an opportunity like this was bound to improve. Once I was a private student – and paying him accordingly – *Sifu* answered my queries and explained them to me with patience.

Siu nim tau, *chum kiu*, *biu tze*, *Drill Wooden Man*, *Dismantle Wooden Man*, *Eight-Chop Knives*, *Six and A Half Point Pole*, and *Tripoles* were all included in my curriculum.

The difference was apparent. *Sifu* personally taught and practiced with me. I had the rare opportunity to learn from and practice with *Sifu* over a period of nearly five years! It must have been *yuan* (緣) – predestined – that I should become a fighter.

"Duncan, how often did you practice?"

"An average of six hours a day, six days a week, during this entire period."

"How much time did you have left for doing homework?"

"None."

"How did you do at school?"

"How do you think? I was appalling!"

Chapter 12

Yip Man's Challenger

Hong Kong
1955

Use the unexpected to win
出 奇 制 勝
(*chu qi zhi sheng*)
The Art of War (孫子兵法)
Sunzi (孫子, 500 B.C.)

Sunzi (also known as Sun Wu, 孫武), a military strategist during the Spring and Autumn Period (770-474 B.C.), was the author of *The Art of War* (孫子兵法, *Sunzi Bingfa*), which is considered the greatest work of all time on military strategy and tactics. It is a companion for generals and a textbook for students of military and business schools around the world. If Confucius is revered as the literary saint of China, then Sunzi is deservedly the military saint.

There is a general opinion, even among *Wing Chun* practitioners, that *Wing Chun* has few kicking techniques. This is a misconception. *Wing Chun* kicks are powerful and destructive when delivered by the handful of those who had the fortune and perseverance to learn the art from *Sifu* Yip Man himself.

There were many stories of *Sifu*'s martial encounters, both in Foshan and Hong Kong, episodes with nicknames like 'bending the barrel of a handgun' and 'breaking wooden pillars with kicks'. *Sifu* did not repeat these stories, which he neither denied nor acknowledged.

When *Sifu* arrived in Hong Kong in 1949, he was destitute and he resorted to teaching *Kung Fu*. In those days, *Wing Chun* was unheard of in Hong Kong. In order to attract students, he had to establish a reputation, and in order to do that he had to show his wares.

There were numerous challengers. Those who were genuinely interested would later become his students, but those who showed signs of contempt would invariably end up on the floor or in the hospital.

A couple of weeks after attending *Sifu*'s studio, I was honored to witness what would later become a common sight in my own studios.

Four or five of us, all new students, were working out when a man in his thirties entered, asking for Yip Man. We thought he was one of the elder *Kung Fu* brothers, for *Sifu* had many senior students who were much older than us.

Sifu was taking his regular afternoon nap in the cubicle behind a curtain. A distinct aroma was emanating from the space, unlike cigarette smoke. Later we would discover what it was and become used to it.

He must have overheard our conversation with the man for he emerged from the cubicle in his white undershirt and long black pants. As he went over to the man, he signaled us to continue practicing. Their conversation didn't last long. He turned around and told us to step aside. Unaware of what was going on, we moved aside and stood against the walls.

Sifu was 62 years old, small in stature and light in weight. He probably measured five-foot-two and weighed 110 pounds. He was gaunt with a penetrating gaze. His gait was typically his own – erect and tilting slightly backward, giving the impression that he was afraid to step forward. When he walked, he landed his heels firmly on the ground. I recall that he once told Bruce Lee in my presence that it was not good to walk with his heels off the ground, a gait unmistakable in Bruce's movies. I learned later that *walking with heels hanging* implies a short life span. Unfortunately, *Sifu* was right about this portent. Bruce Lee died early.

With both arms behind his back, *Sifu* just stood casually on his left foot. He raised his right leg so that his right knee was above his waist and the sole of his right foot was facing the challenger. He gave the impression that he was going to stamp his opponent with the sole of his right foot.

The challenger was much younger, taller, and heavier. In the combative stance he was accustomed to, he raised his arms, clenched his fists tightly and was ready to move in. His horse stance was low, and he sucked in his chest. This was *Zhu's Mantis* (朱家螳螂, *zhu jia tang lang*). He looked impressive just standing there.

Sifu feinted to kick with his right foot and the young man shifted quickly forward, crossed his forearms and tried to block *Sifu's* kick. His intention was to jam the right leg and push it down. He would then charge forward and punch his fists upward to attack *Sifu's* throat.

Before his fists could reach *Sifu's* right leg, *Sifu* had stomped his right foot on the floor abruptly and heavily, avoiding his punches, and simultaneously sprang his left foot upward to stamp the sole on his opponent's chest, sending him flying against the wall. The young challenger fell and landed on the floor, blood spurting from his mouth. *Sifu* told us to carry him out to the street corner, and returned to his cubicle.

"Duncan, why did Yip Man raise his right foot and stand on one foot in preparation?"

"It was a strategy to lure his opponent to attack where he wanted him to attack, and he succeeded. He made his opponent believe he was going to kick with his right foot. In fact it was his left foot which delivered the definitive blow. As Sunzi said, *use the unexpected to win.*"

"Where was the power coming from?"

"From the challenger."

"How is that? The guy was charging forward with so much pace and power, how could he possibly be sent flying in the opposite direction with hardly any effort from a smaller older man?"

"It is not power. The key is the *management* of power. *Wing Chun Eight Kicks* (詠春八腳, *yong chun ba jiao*) is eight ways of exerting kicking power. The one *Sifu* used was *power exertion from leg change* (換　發力, *huan jiao fa li*). It was the leg on the ground, which *sprang out* (彈, *tan*) like the blade of a flick knife, that did the damage."

"Duncan, there is a popular misconception that *Wing Chun* does not have effective kicks."

"That is because *Sifu* told me only a few disciples knew how to kick."

"Why?"

"It was too painful to practice. You have to put up with a lot of pain."

"How did you practice?"

"I had to kick the wooden poles, which was a very painful business."

"When can students start learning?"

"After at least four years of practicing how to apply *Wing Chun* techniques."

Yip Man vs. challenger

Yip feinted a right kick

The challenger tried to block

Yip stomped
his right foot...

...and stamped his left foot into the challenger's chest

Chapter 13

Yip Man's Long Pole

Hong Kong
1955-1959

Standing a hundred paces away
Shoot an arrow through a willow leaf
百 步 穿 楊
(*bai bu chuan yang*)
Zhan Guo Ce (戰國策)
Liu Xiang (劉向)

This idiom is about an archer during the Warring States Period (474-221 B.C.) who could shoot an arrow through a willow leaf a hundred times without fail while standing a hundred paces away. It is now used to describe the skill of an individual who can shoot, pass or throw accurately from a distance.

The *Wing Chun* Long Pole is called *liu dian ban gun* (六點半棍), literally 'six points and a half'. In Chinese it is pronounced 6:30 as in the time of day. The long pole measures seven feet two inches in Chinese measurement, which is about nine feet long.

The long pole is held at the larger end, instead of at the middle. Strength is required just to hold it up, and enormous strength is required to fight with it. Wielded by a skilled user, the long pole is powerful and lethal. Because of its unusual length it is extremely difficult to get close to the holder. On the other hand, its weakness is that once an opponent gets closer than the halfway mark, the holder will be in trouble.

'Six points and a half' signifies the management of power: 'six points' being one's own power, and 'half' the power of one's opponent once he passes the halfway mark of the long pole. The 'half' is designed to defend oneself in desperate situations and is called *Rescue Pole* (救棍, *jiu gun*).

Han Xiang-zi (韓湘子), one of the Eight Immortals of Taoist mythology, was an expert in the art of blowing (吹 *chui*) a bamboo flute (簫 *xiao*), which was held horizontally and parallel to the lips. *Han Xiang-zi chui xiao* is the term used to describe the technique of holding the Rescue Pole, which resembles the way the immortal held the musical instrument.

One day *Sifu*, already 64, was in a particularly good mood and he told a few of us there was something he wanted to demonstrate.

Guan chai ding (棺材釘), special nails, are used to secure coffin lids tightly to the box. Each nail measures about ten inches long and is very difficult to hammer all the way into the wood with one single strike.

With us watching, *Sifu* picked up a coffin nail and pressed the tip against the wall. His other hand held a hammer with which he tapped the head of the nail carefully and gently so that the nail was only an inch perpendicular into the brick wall. He then picked up a long pole and held it horizontally so that the smaller end was almost three feet away from the head of the nail. In one motion, at lightning speed, he shifted in, hammered and buried the whole nail into the brick wall with the long pole while holding the far end!

At the moment of contact the long pole had to be horizontal and parallel to the ground, and the tip of the pole hammered the head of the nail at exactly the correct angle. This feat, which I saw with my own eyes, would be impossible for me, or anyone I know, to repeat.

Chapter 14

YIP MAN – NOT GRANDMASTER

A Man of Two Cities
Grandmaster of Neither

In Chinese chess, Grandmaster is the title reserved for national champions. There have been only ten grandmasters since 1955, when the first official National Chess Championship Competition was held.

In *Kung Fu*, Grandmaster is the title strictly reserved for the leader of a style. Like the succession in a dynasty, there is only one leader in each generation. Before a leader dies, he selects a disciple to succeed him.

Yip Man was 13 when he became the disciple of Chen Hua-shun (陳華順), the Grandmaster and sole leader of the Fifth Generation, who passed away when Yip Man was still in his teens. The mantle of leadership passed to Chen Ro-mian (陳汝綿), the eldest son of Chen Hua-shun, who became the sole leader and Grandmaster of the Sixth Generation.

Yip Man was not the leader of a style, and therefore he did not assume the title of Grandmaster. Nor was he entitled to select a successor to lead *Wing Chun Kung Fu*. While he did not claim the title, he also failed to disclaim it when he was addressed as Grandmaster. His failure to do so caused confusion as far as leadership and succession were concerned.

It has been suggested that Yip Man should be considered the Grandmaster of the First Generation in Hong Kong (usually by those who wish to call themselves grandmasters). If this were the case, where would Liang Bi, who taught him in Hong Kong, be placed? In any event, Yip Man would hardly divorce himself from the ancestral *Wing Chun* family in Foshan just to form his own family in Hong Kong in order to call himself the Grandmaster. Yip Man was a very traditional man and would never name a successor to a title to which was not his to bestow.

Today a profusion of so-called *Wing Chun* grandmasters crowd the market. The unsuspecting public is led to believe each is the designated disciple and therefore the leader of the generation. However, this is far from the truth, and is an unethical ruse for the purpose of attracting gullible students.

By the foregoing logic, Yip Man's disciples were similarly ineligible for the title of Grandmaster. Despite his accomplishments and proficiency in the art of *Wing Chun Kung Fu,* Duncan Leung refuses to be inappropriately addressed as Grandmaster.

The present disorganization of *Wing Chun Kung Fu* is partially to blame for the confusion regarding the term 'Grandmaster'. One way out of this morass might be to reserve the title 'Grandmaster' for the leader of *Wing Chun*, as is traditionally the case, and the lesser title 'grandmaster' for the elite practitioners of the art – the genuine experts. 'The Grandmaster' might be elected instead of selected as was the case in former times. It is not necessarily the best *Wing Chun* fighter who should assume the leadership. Perhaps in this day and age, the art is best served by the election of an able administrator who can command the respect of the *Wing Chun* family as Grandmaster. Additionally, perhaps a council, rather than a single individual, should lead and oversee the much-needed revival of *Wing Chun Kung Fu.*

2008 is the 36th anniversary of Yip Man's death. It is time to leave the spirit of the Old Man in peace. Those who knew him understand that he would be much happier to be remembered as the greatest of the Sixth Generation of the ancestral *Wing Chun* family in Foshan than as a fictitious Grandmaster of an artificially created First Generation of Hong Kong.

Chapter 15

I Run For My Life

Hong Kong
1958

Escape is the best stratagem
三 十 六 着 走 為 上 着
(*san shi liu zhao, zou wei shang zhao*)
Water Margin (水滸傳)
Shi Nai-an (施耐庵)

Shi Nai-an was an author of the Ming Dynasty (1368-1644) who wrote *Water Margin* (水滸傳 *shui hu zhuan*), one of the Four Classical Chinese Novels. Very little is known about him. It is alleged that Luo Guan-zhong (羅貫中), author of *Romance of the Three Kingdoms,* was his pupil, and Luo could well be the legitimate author of *Water Margin.*

The 36 Stratagems recounts the stories of the best-known strategies used by tacticians to outwit and outmaneuver their enemies throughout Chinese history.

The 36th stipulates: *Escape is the best stratagem* (三十六着 走為上着). To escape does not imply cowardice. One elects to avoid a situation which is not winnable, without subjecting oneself unnecessarily to jeopardy. Thereby, losses can be minimized; one can then regroup and try again. One learns to flee before learning to fight. When life is at stake, run if one cannot defeat the opponent. The same strategies apply in non-combat situations; for example, in business, avoid conflict if one cannot overcome the competition. The wisest know when to quit the field of battle.

It was a lovely Hong Kong afternoon. The weather was perfect and Duncan was in an expansive mood. Once more queuing in line for a movie ticket, he was looking forward to the picture, a popular hit.

The Oriental Theatre was situated at the southwest corner of Fleming Road and Thomson Road in Wan Chai (灣仔), a district frequented by sailors and tourists alike because of the famous Suzie Wong.

Duncan was far back in a long queue for the 5:30p.m. show. At the back of the queue the touts were most active. Although there was an imposing Indian guard replete with a turban who was supposed to maintain order, he didn't dare bother the touts who tended to be triad members.

"Tickets! Tickets! Why wait in the queue? Only two dollars each." A couple of touts were soliciting prospective customers. Back stall tickets were selling for $1.20 each at the booth, but there were people willing to pay the extra eighty cents to avoid the disappointment of tickets being sold out. All the touts' tickets were sold within minutes.

As Duncan was getting closer to the ticket booth, these two touts jumped into the queue right in front of him with the intention buying more tickets to sell at the back. Duncan, understandably angry, told them to get out of the line.

They turned around and delivered a common Cantonese expletive: "Fuck your mother!"

"You should not jump the queue."

Again cursing Duncan, "Fuck your mother. Haven't you died before?" one of them tried to push him – a big mistake.

As broadminded as Duncan was, he was not about to permit such an insult to go unpunished. As he assumed a fighting posture, he thought to himself that if his mother only knew how filial and protective he was, she would certainly have spoiled him even more.

The thugs spread out, one on either side of Duncan. Wordlessly ("I always fight without uttering a word. If you want to fight why bother saying anything at all?"), he walked towards the tout on his left, who struck out with his right fist at Duncan's face. Using a *guan sau* (摑手) for the first punch, Duncan then immediately *covered* his left swing with a *lop sau* (攞手) while simultaneously using his left hand to hook his assailant's neck, pulling him around and flinging him away to land roughly face down on the ground.

Turning, the other tout was charging in an attempt to grab Duncan in a bear hug. His outspread arms gave Duncan the opening to launch a left arrow punch followed by a vicious right punch and a solid kick to his solar plexus.

The spectators were amazed to watch a kid knock down two guys and some even applauded. Duncan, feeling he had handled the situation well and basking in the approval of the crowd, stood back in line for the movie.

Suddenly, he heard: Pang! Pang! Pang! It was the sound of breaking glass. He wheeled around, and to his horror saw at least twenty men, wielding broken soda bottles and charging furiously. Terrified, Duncan turned and fled. He dared not even look back. He raced along Hennessy Road toward Causeway Bay. Duncan ran and ran until he could run no more. Finally, out of breath, at

Queen Victoria's statue inside Victoria Park, he rested, panting. His pursuers were nowhere to be seen. They had given up. After all, the distance was well over 2000 meters. Leaning against the stature, bile rushed up his throat and he threw up. God save the Queen! God save ME!

"Duncan, were you looking for fights in those days? It sounds as though you would brawl at the slightest provocation "

"Yes, you're right. In those days we were looking for opportunities to fight. This was the only way we could practice and find out how good we were."

"Did your *Sifu* know about it?"

"Are you kidding? He encouraged us to go out and fight."

"I thought *Kung Fu* was supposed to be for self-defense."

"Offense is the best defense, right? Joking aside, *Wing Chun* teaches you how to attack when your opponent defends, and how to counter-attack before your opponent's attack can reach you. "

"Duncan, you mentioned the word *chase* before. What is it?"

"*Chase* in *Wing Chun* means follow-up. Once your opponent is down or on the defensive with your first punch or kick, you do not allow him to recover; otherwise the fight starts all over again. The principle of the *chase* is that once you get your opponent on the defensive, you never let up until he is finished. This is one of the reasons why *Wing Chun* can be so effective against a larger and stronger opponent. In *Wing Chun,* we give the opponent no opportunity to recover from his retreat."

Chapter 16

First Stab

Hong Kong
1958

Bare hands against a knife
空 手 入 白 刃
(*kong shou ru bai ren*)

Fighting barehanded against a knife is considered the most difficult thing in martial arts. To disarm an attacker wielding a knife requires confidence, speed and good fighting techniques. However, no matter how good and how careful you are, unforeseen accidents can occur...

After three years of learning how to apply *Wing Chun* and being involved in numerous combat situations, Duncan was so self-confident that he thought nothing of taking on several opponents simultaneously.

During the 1950s, going to cinemas and parties was popular entertainment for students. Elvis Presley, the King of Rock 'n' Roll, had teenagers the whole world over gyrating to his rhythms. In Hong Kong his music and movies were all the rage.

Duncan and his friend Bruce Lee were no exception to the rock 'n' roll craze. He and Bruce took dancing lessons from Lesley, a singer and bass guitarist in a nightclub band. Lesley was very good, and until Bruce left Hong Kong for America in 1958, the two boys enjoyed alternating between the two studios, learning fighting at one and dancing at the other. They were proud of their achievements in both.

One day, after watching a movie at the Gala Theatre on Lockhart Road in Wan Chai (by now, it should be apparent that Duncan was a great fan of the cinema), he took a short cut to Gordon Road. Coming from the other end of the narrow path were seven or eight guys in their early twenties. They were talking and laughing coarsely. They were pushing each other playfully, leaving hardly any room for other pedestrians to pass. They appeared to have just left a party, and looked like teddy boys from the way they dressed and behaved. Duncan wanted to provoke them.

"Shut your mouths," he taunted as he approached them.

A few of them swore in unison. Then they blocked the passage, stopping him from passing.

Their superiority in numbers was obvious, and the first one took advantage of it, trying to push Duncan, who slapped his outstretched arm down with one hand (right *pak sau*) and punched his face with the other. One more punch to the chest and he was on the ground. Sensing another guy was attacking him from his right, Duncan turned around and saw this guy throwing a straight punch at him. Shifting immediately to his attacker's right side, Duncan *covered* the right punch with a right *tan sau* (攤手) and punched his chest with the other. Duncan then launched a series of chain punches that floored him.

But when Duncan turned to face the rest of the group, someone brandished a switchblade. Instinctively, Duncan *covered*, and the teddy boy slashed with the knife even as Duncan stomped heavily on his chest with his right foot. As he fell, Duncan's opponent unintentionally stabbed the knife into the back of Duncan's right knee, where it remained stuck. Duncan fell to the ground, twitching in pain.

In one sense, he was lucky because all the teddy boys had scurried away, or he would have become a human punchbag. Duncan asked an onlooker to call his home for assistance. The family chauffeur arrived and drove Duncan to the nearest clinic to have the knife removed.

"Duncan, did the doctor give you a local anesthetic during the procedure?"

"No way. I hate needles, remember?"

"I thought you were so good then. Why didn't you disarm him?"

"I had not yet learned to fight with a knife or disarm a knife-wielding opponent. Fighting against an opponent from behind with a knife while beating his accomplice was considerably more difficult. Face to face, it wasn't a problem."

"So when did you start learning the art of fighting with knives?"

"Believe me, right after this."

Chapter 17

Young Swordsman

Hong Kong
1959

Able to apply what one learns is joy
學 而 時 習 之 不 亦 樂 乎
(*xue er shi xi zhi, bu yi le fu*)
The Analects of Confucius
Confucius

When Confucius wrote the *Analects*, he meant his disciples and students should be joyful when they could apply what they learned in approaching the ideal of the superior man (君子, *jun zi*) – a person whose character embodies the virtue of benevolence and whose acts are in accordance with the rites and correct behavior. He certainly did not intend that one could derive joy from causing another man agony.

Eight-Chop Knives (八斬刀, *ba zhan dao*) are short and heavy. They are modified from the eleven-and-a-half inch long *Butterfly Knives* (蝴蝶刀, *hu die dao*) used by different *Kung Fu* styles. The *Eight-Chop Knife* is unique in its design. The blade is narrower than a regular butterfly knife and its handle is tilted about five degrees downward from the blade. These modifications enable the user not only to chop, but also to pierce. Piercing with a short knife is unique in *Wing Chun*. Wrist strength and flexibility are essential and necessary to manipulate the knives effectively. There are eight major movements to the form, and each movement has its own follow-up techniques. The knives are used in pairs and they are often referred to as *Double Knives* (雙刀, *shuang dao*). To carry and fight with them was as illegal in 1959 as it is today.

In the late 1950s and early 1960s, the now-defunct Pan Am was one of the world's major airlines. Carrying a Pan Am traveling bag to school was fashionable among students. Normally, books, sporting shirts, shoes, and other miscellaneous school items were packed in it, but Duncan packed a pair of double knives in his Pan Am traveling bag when he went to school. He had watched many Chinese *Kung Fu* movies about virtuous and chivalrous swordsmen and their righteous deeds in different dynasties. In those epics, swordsmen (and swordswomen) roamed the land carrying different kinds of weapons, including swords, knives, spears, axes, and so on.

Not only could they fight skillfully and efficiently with their chosen weapons, they could outrun and out-jump Olympic and world record holders. Not only could they smash rocks and pillars into pieces with punches and kicks, they could even fly! The unusual skills and extraordinary maneuvers of these superhuman beings made you wonder where all the secret *Kung Fu* menus were.

This young swordsman was more realistic because his *Sifu* had not taught him the art of defying the pull of gravity. He could only run and jump like an ordinary human being, but he could fight, with or without weapons, like few people could. He roamed the streets of Hong Kong, looking for hawkers and tradesmen who were skilled in the handling of knives…

One day shortly after the Chinese New Year holidays, while I was wandering along a street in Sham Shui Po, I was attracted to a fruit stall, and I was not the only one. There were other spectators crowding around, admiring the skill and speed with which the hawker was peeling pears. His technique was not unusual. Many other hawkers knew it, but few could match his speed and neatness. Holding a sharp watermelon knife in one hand and a pear in the other, he was flicking his knife and peeling the skin longitudinally. He undressed the pear in seconds. Dangling the pear by its stalk, he basked in the admiration of the crowd which rewarded him with oohs and aahs.

But I could not help opening my big mouth to shout: "What's so exceptional about that? Can you fight with it?"

"Get lost, kid," said the vendor, who then proceeded to yell some nasty names at me.

"OK, let's fight," I said.

He took the bait. "Kid, I am going to chop you up." Holding the watermelon knife, he made a chopping gesture.

Watermelon knives are the favorite tools of fruit hawkers for chopping and peeling fruits. They are thin and light with a blunt end. The blade is about a foot long and sharpened so often that it arches in the middle. They are also favored by triad members for fighting because they are light and easy to hide.

"Come on, try me," I dared him, as I withdrew my prized knives from my Pan Am bag. Although I am ashamed when I think back on it today, I should mention that I had gained some measure of proficiency with the knives by practicing on dogs. These were stray dogs, but dogs nonetheless. I had not yet developed the American sensibility that Rover is man's best friend. (And even though I have long since given it up, in those days, I still thought dog was some of the best-tasting meat around.)

The vendor was absolutely stunned to see the knives, and so were the spectators! In the past, I had had a number of opportunities to fight with knives in similar situations. But each time, I had backed off because of fear. I wasn't yet confident in my own ability and skill in the use of the *Eight-Chop Knives*. This time, however, I had no choice. The vendor was actually chopping at me.

I was just an excited kid, and my reflexes kicked in. I used my double knife to knock his knife to the ground. Then I waved my knife in front of his face to taunt him: "Come on, pick it up!" At this point, he completely lost his temper and came at me in earnest. I blocked with one hand and cut him in the midriff with the other. Terrified of what I had done and of the potential consequences, I fled. When I cautiously went back and peeked from around a corner, I saw an ambulance had arrived. I checked the newspaper every day for a report of the incident and prayed he wouldn't die.

To this day, I do not know whether the vendor survived or not. I certainly hope so. I vowed then never to use the knives in public again.

This was the second time I ran for my life.

Chapter 18

BRUCE LEE AND I BEATEN

Hong Kong
1958

Subdue the dragon, tame the tiger
降 龍 伏 虎
(*xiang long fu hu*)
Journey to the West (西遊記)
Wu Cheng-en (吳承恩, c.1500-1582)

Wu Cheng-en was an author of the Ming Dynasty (1368-1644) who wrote *Journey to the West* (西遊記, *xi you ji*), one of the four classical Chinese novels.

In Buddhist mythology, there were two Buddhist arhats (羅漢 *luo han* – an eminent monk who has achieved enlightenment), one of whom subdued a dragon with incantations and the other who tamed a tiger with an abbot's staff (錫杖 *xi zhang*). The saying '*Subdue the dragon and tame the tiger*' is often used to describe the ability of an individual to overcome powerful adversaries. In China, the tiger is considered the king of the animal kingdom, and the Chinese character for tiger is invariably associated with brave generals (虎將 *hu jiang*) and warriors.

It may be hard to believe, but one day Bruce Lee and Duncan Leung were beaten one after the other on the same day by a seasoned pugilist. It did happen. It was when they were young and inexperienced – as the Chinese would say, when *they did not know the height of heaven or the thickness of the earth* (不知天高地厚, *bu zhi tian gao di hou*).

Out of respect to past and living *Kung Fu* masters, the author chooses not to reveal the names, *Kung Fu* styles or the triumphant episodes against them between 1955 and 1959. The following episode is a revelation of how two *Wing Chun* greats, the dragon and the tiger, were defeated by a *Cai Li Fo* (蔡李佛) master when they were both young and inexperienced, and how the tiger took his revenge when he returned two weeks later.

After taking private lessons with *Sifu* for over two years, I thought I was pretty good. And indeed I was, although maybe not as good as I believed. Fellow students and I roamed the streets, looking for opportunities to fight. We had become bored simply because fighting against people who didn't know much *Kung Fu* no longer had any appeal. We needed greater challenges.

We became bold and began venturing into *Kung Fu* studios to test our *Wing Chun* against different *Kung Fu* styles. Our ruse was simple. Still in our uniforms after school, we would go into a studio and ask to see the head instructor. Eager to recruit new students and anxious to impress, the unsuspecting instructor would glorify the effectiveness of his style and usually exaggerate his own expertise. He could not wait to demonstrate what he could do.

We'd pretend to be interested and say something like: "The forms look good, but I've heard about this *Wing Chun*. I wonder if yours is any good against that." The instructor would invariably reply: "Of course. What is *Wing Chun* any way? Let me show you." Thereby he fell into our trap, and a free fight ensued.

Sometimes we would just enroll in the school, pay the initial fee, and start learning. Usually it was the elder *Kung Fu* brothers who initiated us. After a couple of lessons we would question the effectiveness of the style and his expertise. And then a fight would follow.

We were never sure of the outcome. Some instructors were humbled for daring to pit their knowledge and expertise against ours. But we had our fair share of defeats. Our overblown confidence, arrogance, and contempt did not go unpunished. Against elder brothers we rarely lost. But, one time, Bruce Lee and I wandered into a studio and were given a lesson we would never forget.

At our school there were a couple of Eurasian brothers – twins actually – who were learning *Cai Li Fo* (or *Choi Lei Fut,* 蔡李佛). They were not good enough to give Bruce or me meaningful resistance, but they dared us to go to the studio to meet their *Sifu*, and we were more than happy to accept that invitation.

Bruce, another schoolmate named Caesar, and a couple more of us went to the studio. Their *Sifu* was in his forties and about my height and size, confident-looking and very polite. He asked who would like to try first. Self-confident and proud of himself, Bruce stepped forward.

Cai Li Fo, like *Wing Chun*, also comes from Foshan, the capital of *Kung Fu*. It is an established style, known for swinging fully extended arms and legs. *Wing Chun* attacks and defends along and from the centerline, while *Cai Li Fo* attacks from the sides and deliberately exposes the front to attack.

Unfamiliar with the intricacies of his opponent's style, Bruce charged forward, throwing *chain punches* to the exposed chest. The seasoned instructor just took one step backward, easily avoiding the punches. Before Bruce's right punch could reach his chest, the *Sifu* leaned slightly backward on his left foot, struck Bruce's right forearm with his extended left forearm, and swung his right foot toward Bruce's leading left leg. While Bruce's right punch was knocked aside, the *Cai Li Fo* man's vicious kick struck Bruce's calf, bent his knee and sent him tumbling to the ground.

Bruce's defeat did not deter me. I took my turn eagerly, but more cautiously. I feinted a kick to my opponent's right with my left foot. He stepped backward on his right foot and at the same time swung at me with his right fist, forcing me to *cover*. I *covered* with a left *tan sau* (攤手), but when my left forearm met his advancing arm, it suddenly twisted like a snake over the top of my *tan sau*, punching downward and forward. His right fist landed heavily on my chest and shook me. After hitting my chest with his right fist, he swung the same arm backward in a circle, and the back of his right fist hit the left side of my jaw. Then he swung his left arm at me, which caught the right side of my partially covered neck. It was lucky that my forearms partially blocked the impact on my neck, or I might have been seriously injured. Before I could even balance myself, the twins' *Sifu* followed up with a left kick, which sent me flying to the floor.

Bruce and I got up, dusted ourselves off, and slunk out of the *Cai Li Fo* studio.

When I told *Sifu* what had happened, he was extremely displeased and said repeatedly: "You deserved the punishment. You should have asked me before going there. Each style has its own advantages and disadvantages. If you know what they are, then you shouldn't lose."

He quoted from *The Art of War*, which was written more than 2500 years ago by Sunzi, the great Chinese strategist: *Know your enemy and know yourself, and you can fight a hundred battles without defeat* (知彼知己 百戰不殆, *zhi bi zhi ji bai zhan bu dai*). I have never forgotten this quotation. *Sifu* went on to point out the strengths and weaknesses of *Cai Li Fo* and other styles and taught me how to counter them.

Two weeks later I returned to the studio. Somewhat surprised that I was back so soon after my humiliation, the master knew I was prepared and serious.

Sifu cautioned that against a *Cai Li Fo* expert, I must not charge forward rapidly. I should only inch forward carefully and wait for the right moment. Therefore, I now waited for him to make the first move.

When the master swung his fully extended right arm at me this time, I *covered* with both arms with a *guan sau* while stepping half a pace forward to the left to meet his advancing arm. His right forearm struck my forearms, but he could not twist this time, because I had *covered* with both arms, not only avoiding his extended twist and punch, but also nullifying his power.

The very moment after our arms met, I turned my horse to the right to *cover* my right side, the exposed area he was mostly likely to attack. While taking a step forward with my right foot, I raised my right forearm to *cover* any strike from his left arm. As expected, he followed up with a full swing with his left arm, trying to strike me from my right. But it was too late for him. Before his left forearm could meet my raised right forearm, I had already taken a right step forward, literally walking into him. The moment his left forearm met my right forearm, I had already bent down at my right knee joint and swept the right side of his chest simultaneously with my left elbow. When it landed on target I could hear ribs cracking. He was lying on the floor when I left.

Bruce Lee vs. the *Cai Li Fo* master

Bruce Lee attacked with chain punches

The master struck and kicked

Bruce Lee landed on the floor

Duncan Leung vs. the *Cai Li Fo* master

Leung *covered* with *tan sau*

The master twisted right punch over *tan sau*...

...and struck Leung's chest...

Two weeks later, Leung returned

He *covered* the right swing with a *guan sau*...

...*covered* the left swing, took a right step forward, bent his right knee...

...and swept his left elbow, which landed on the master's chest

Chapter 19

Bruce Lee and the Wooden Man

Leave fragrance for a hundred generations
Leave a stink for ten thousand years
流 芳 百 世 遺 臭 萬 年
(*liu fang bai shi yi chou wan nian*)
Zi Zhi Tong Jian (資治通鑑)
Sima Guang (司馬光, 1019-1086)

Sima Guang was a historian of the Song Dynasty (960-1279). His *Zi Zhi Tong Jian*, which covered a period between 403 B.C. and A.D. 959, has been favorite reading for many rulers over the centuries, including even Mao Zedong, because of its emphasis on politics and militarism.

Individuals leave their mark on history in various ways. Some men leave fragrance and some an unsavory aroma. Long after his death, Bruce Lee is still the most recognizable Chinese person in the world. Will his fragrance last for a hundred generations? Only time will tell. *Wing Chun* practitioners who think they are well versed in *Wooden Man* may have second thoughts after reading the following story.

Bruce Lee's part in the American TV series *The Green Hornet* had caught the attention of television audiences worldwide. It would not be inaccurate to say he was the first person to popularize martial arts through the medium of television. *Karate* was emerging at the time, and *Kung Fu* was unheard of. The fact that a Chinese had to hide behind a mask with a Japanese name, Kato, reflected the obscurity of *Kung Fu* in the West.

Kung Fu is the Cantonese term for Chinese martial arts, which was first employed and made popular by Bruce Lee in his interviews and demonstrations. Now the term *Kung Fu* is in standard dictionaries and has become part of our normal lexicon.

With his newfound popularity and success, Bruce Lee returned to Hong Kong and made an impact of unexpected magnitude. His *Kung Fu* prowess was awesome, and people admired and loved him because his *Kung Fu* was genuine. Until his time, *Kung Fu* had been looked upon with derision, a fiction valid only in Chinese action movies. Now, it began to be taken seriously. Bruce Lee was restoring it as a significant cultural and artistic contribution of China to the world.

Because of him, *Wing Chun* was catapulted onto the world stage and has since become one of the most practiced (as well as abused) martial arts in the world. At the same time, his *Sifu*, Yip Man, was also elevated to the zenith of his career.

With fame and fortune Bruce Lee returned to Hong Kong and paid a visit to his *Sifu*, imploring Yip Man to teach him the art of *Dismantle Wooden Man* (拆樁 *chai zhuang*), meaning 'breaking it down'. *Drill Wooden Man* (上樁 *shang zhuang*) is the practice of the 108 techniques with the *Wooden Man*. It is relatively easy, and many *Wing Chun* practitioners are conversant with these. *Dismantle Wooden Man*, however, is the actual application of the techniques – fighting with the *Wooden Man*. It is extremely difficult, and is known only to a few of Yip Man's formal disciples. Bruce Lee knew *Drill Wooden Man,* but had not been taught how to dismantle, which is the actual application aspect. Many *Wing Chun* practitioners either don't have an instructor who can and will train them in this; the majority do not even realize the essential component they are missing. But Bruce Lee did. He was aware of this gap in his martial arts education. He knew that without learning *Dismantle Wooden Man,* the mastery of applied fighting techniques of *Wing Chun* was illusory.

Bruce Lee offered Yip Man a large sum of money – enough to buy an apartment for his retirement. His *Sifu* declined. One author, Leung Ting, alleged that Yip Man revealed to him that Bruce Lee had made a disrespectful remark, which upset Yip Man sufficiently for him to refuse the offer. 斬斷窮根 (*zhan duan qiong gen*) literally means *sever the root of poverty*, which can be interpreted as a disrespectful remark, depending upon the context in which it is offered. Some people would take it as an insult.

Bruce Lee offered another explanation. He told Duncan: "*Sifu* said: '*Dismantle Wooden Man* is very strenuous. I am too old and do not have the stamina to teach you. Learn from one of my private disciples.'" But Bruce Lee had too much pride to learn from anyone but Yip Man.

There are people who like to put down others in order to elevate themselves. Worse are those who metaphorically trample over dead bodies in order to accrue self-glory. When Bruce was alive, some martial artists claimed he had refused their challenges because he was scared of them. After he died, hypocrites bragged that they could have defeated him easily had he lived, and some even made delusional claims that they had beaten him. But Bruce Lee was, in reality, one of the greatest fighters in modern history. Today, his popularity remains undiminished, and his image is easily recognized. Peace to his soul.

Above: Yip Man having tea in a Hong Kong restaurant in 1957 after his daily training with Duncan Leung.

Left: Duncan just before his departure for Australia in 1959.

Below: Playing the guitar at Townsville Grammar School.

Above: *Sifu* Duncan Leung demonstrating Eight-Chop Knives in 1974.

Below: Duncan shows how to *cover* a 'roundhouse kick'.

Above: Duncan was appointed instructor to the Norfolk police in 1978.

Below: At a presentation by the Virginia Port Authority.

Left: Duncan Leung outside his first *Wing Chun* studio at No.3 Great Jones Street, New York, 1974.

Below: At a martial arts event in Germany.

Duncan and his victorious students at New York's Madison Square Garden for the 1975 Full Contact Free Fight Championships. Joe Young (below) took the heavyweight trophy.

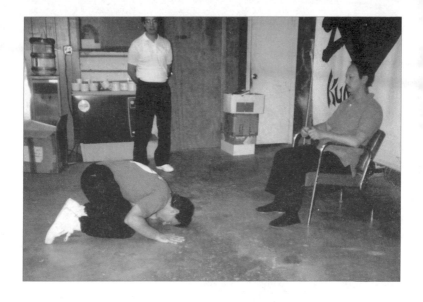

Rohy Batliwala went through the ritual of *three kneels, nine kowtows* to become a formal disciple of *Sifu* Duncan Leung in 1988. Rohy later won the Full Contact Championships in Hong Kong.

Duncan's most dedicated disciple, Steve Falkner, in training with Rohy
Batliwala and a professional Thai boxer.

Duncan Leung with the Virginia Beach SWAT team.

With the SWAT team in 1998.

Bruce Lee is remembered by people around the world, and his memory is honored by a bronze statue on the waterfront of Tsim Sha Tsui, Hong Kong, which was unveiled in 2005.

Down Under

The latter part of the 1950s and early 1960s witnessed the beginning of the exodus of Hong Kong students to study abroad. Their favorite destinations were English-speaking countries such as the United States, Great Britain, Australia and Canada. What had started off as a trickle for the privileged had gathered momentum and soon the floodgates were open for students whose parents could afford to send them, because the Hong Kong economy had begun to grow rapidly and continued to prosper.

At that time, Hong Kong University was the only recognized institution in the colony which provided higher education. Those who met the stringent admission requirements and successfully matriculated were considered part of the elite.

Gaining admission to Hong Kong University was extremely difficult because of stiff competition for the limited number of places. And gaining admission to matriculation classes was no easier. Students who did not rate their chances of gaining admission would go to high schools abroad in order to get into foreign universities. There were agencies which specialized in placing students in high schools abroad. However, it should not be assumed that the best and brightest always stayed at home. Over the years there were many outstanding Hong Kong students who studied abroad and who graduated from some of the most prestigious universities and institutes. Some remained and integrated into the societies of their respective countries; and others returned to offer valuable contributions to Hong Kong. The Chief Executive of Hong Kong is such an example.

For the first time in his life, Duncan felt an urge to improve himself scholastically. However, because of his previous less-than-stellar academic record, his chances of matriculating in Hong Kong were slender. He decided to apply to a high school in Australia, although he actually had no idea at the time where the continent was even located. His choice was interesting. The daughter of his cousin, the actress, had teased him one day about not being able to read the English word *Welcome* on their doormat, despite having taken English at school. He felt so humiliated that he resolved to learn English.

Going to the Australian Consulate for advice, Duncan was asked a routine question by a junior officer: "Why do you want to study in Australia?"

"Is there anything wrong with Australia?"

The officer, looking over Duncan's transcripts, said in Cantonese: "Your school is a very good one, but your reports are not terribly good."

"The school is good, but I'm no good. That is exactly the reason why I have to go. If my reports were any good, I might as well stay in Hong Kong. But with the friends I have, it's too easy for me to play around and not study. I have to leave Hong Kong."

The officer thought for a moment, and then replied: "All right. I'm going to give you a chance. I like your determination, and that's a good start. Let me see how you do. Don't disappoint me."

Chapter 20

Initiation

Townsville

1959

Tiger on the plain bullied by dogs
虎 落 平 川 被 犬 欺
(*hu luo ping chuan bei quan qi*)
Shuo Yue Quan Zhuan (說岳全傳)
Qian Cai (錢彩)

Shuo Yue Quan Zhuan, written by Qian Cai during the Qing Dynasty (1644-1911), is a novel set during the Song Dynasty (960-1279). General Yue Fei (岳飛, 1103-1142) was well known for the four Chinese characters *jing chong bao guo* (精忠報國) tattooed on his back by his mother to remind him of loyalty to his country. His martial valor and military success were legendary, as are the tragic circumstances of his downfall. How ironic that this most loyal general, together with his entire clan, was executed for treason based upon a false accusation by counselors close to the emperor.

In Chinese culture, the dragon is associated with kings and emperors, while tigers are associated with generals and warriors. *Tiger General* is an honorific bestowed upon great generals and warriors. But tigers are mountain animals. When a tiger leaves the mountain for the open plain, even a dog can bully him. The idiom indicates that in unfamiliar territory even a mighty warrior is vulnerable.

In October 1959, Duncan left Hong Kong by sea for Australia. His mother had packed everything he could possibly need in seven large trunks. It was the first time he had left home, much less left his homeland to live on a different continent. While Duncan had been ready to venture into a wider world than he had known during his cloistered childhood, nevertheless he missed his family. All in all, he felt very strange.

His destination – Townsville Grammar School – was a boarding school located in a small town in the state of Queensland. Duncan was the lone Chinese student in the entire school, some of whom had never even seen a Chinese person before.

'Hazing' is a typical rite of passage for new students at university and even at some high schools. The rituals can be friendly and relatively harmless. However, on occasion they can be ugly and downright dangerous.

After welcome speeches by the headmaster and teachers in the assembly hall, each student was given a slip of paper assigning them to various classrooms. Duncan's form master, who taught mathematics and was responsible for training cadets, was an American who had served in the army during the Second World War. He came into the classroom, introduced himself and told the students to get acquainted with one another. He himself went over to a group of older students, and after a little while, he left the classroom.

No sooner had the door swung shut behind the form master, than some students started moving desks and chairs and placing them against the walls, leaving a space in the middle of the classroom.

Eight or ten elder students lined up on one side of the classroom. Not only new but with a poor command of English, Duncan had no idea what was going on.

A student brought in two pairs of boxing gloves and, going over to Duncan, said: "Hey, Jap, come over here!" He had assumed Duncan was Japanese.

The boy pulled the gloves over Duncan's hands and tied the strings. It was the first time he had ever worn boxing gloves. It was a strange feeling. Duncan thought it might be a game. While he was getting used to the new sensation of the gloves, the first in line of the old boys had put on a pair.

Suddenly, Duncan was pushed into the center of the makeshift ring to face his first opponent, a boy much taller and bigger then he. (Later, he was told the boy weighed 20 stones, more than twice Duncan's weight.)

Facing Duncan, his weighty opponent raised his gloves and jabbed. Dodging, Duncan knew it wasn't a game. Continuing to move forward, feinting and throwing jabs, the kid meant business. Without warning, the kid threw a straight punch to Duncan's face. Duncan's *Wing Chun* instincts kicked in; he *covered* and punched him squarely in the face.

At first, Duncan did not follow up, nor did he use anything like full power in returning punches. But the kid kept coming forward, and Duncan realized it would not end unless he hit him harder. When the next hook came, Duncan *covered* and cut his lips with his next punch. Neither of them was wearing a mouth guard, and the boy's lips started bleeding. He stopped fighting, shook Duncan's hand and patted him on the back, acknowledging Duncan's superiority. Then he gave his gloves to the student second in line.

The second in line was shorter but very stocky. Nevertheless, he did not put up too much resistance. This time Duncan smashed his nose, which bled profusely. That ended the round and the gloves were passed to number three.

The third was even easier. He didn't know much about fighting, and when a blow to his face occasioned a bloody nose, he quickly yielded his position to number four.

The fourth actually knew how to fight. He was smart, too. He covered his face with his right forearm in front of him, with his right palm facing outward. Duncan couldn't hit his face, but his right flank was in full view. So Duncan switched tactics. He hooked his stomach with a left fist and, as the body doubled up, followed with a straight right punch to the sternum. The student dropped to the ground breathless. The others helped him up and took off his gloves.

The rest did not dare to carry it further. They crowded around Duncan, congratulating him. They were shocked because he had just whipped members of the school boxing team!

"You are very good. What kind of boxing was that?"

"Chinese *Kung Fu*."

As a result, Duncan was invited to join the boxing team and participated in inter-school competitions and tournaments, helping the school win numerous trophies. He won by knockdowns in every engagement, but was frequently disqualified because of the ferocity of Wing Chun, which the officials didn't understand.

The Aussie boys respected Duncan, and he felt the same for them. Unlike the Chinese, who might gang up against you for revenge, the Australians were good losers. They would come forward and fight one at a time, and when they lost there were no hard feelings.

Chapter 21

THE LONGEST FIGHT

Sydney
1961

Unyielding, unbending
不 屈 不 撓
(*bu qu bu nao*)
Xunzi (荀子, 313-238 B.C.)

Xunzi was a noted philosopher and educationist of the Warring States Period (447-221 B.C). The above quote is actually shorthand for *jian gang er bu qu yi ye* (堅剛而不屈義也), meaning 'unyielding to oppression is the right thing to do' and *zhe er bu nao yong ye* (折而不撓勇也) – 'unbending to adversity is courage'.

After a few months at Townsville Grammar School, Duncan was bored. He wrote to his friends in Hong Kong, extolling the virtues of life in Australia and suggesting they join him. Some accepted the invitation, and life improved.

A year later Duncan and his friends all left Townsville and went to Waverley College in Ladies Mount in Sydney, closer to his other friends who went to school in St. Mary's, a suburb of Sydney. Every Sunday the circle of friends would gather there to play soccer.

One Saturday evening, Lawrence called urgently from St. Mary's:

"Duncan, Jeffrey was beaten up and he is in hospital."

"What happened?"

"Just call William Cheung. We need him to help us."

"William is not in town."

"Then leave a message for him to call me."

William Cheung and Bruce Lee had gone to the same school, and it was William who had introduced Bruce to *Sifu* Yip Man in 1954. (That makes William Cheung Duncan's elder *Kung Fu* brother.) William has lived in Sydney, Australia since the 1950s. Duncan had known him there and last saw him in Virginia Beach in the 1990s.

Duncan hopped on the first train on Sunday morning and arrived at St. Mary's Railway Station. Lawrence and eight of his classmates were there to take him to the hospital to visit Jeffrey. Apparently, the incident had occurred on Friday night. Seven or eight Chinese boys had gone to one of the local pubs near St. Mary's Railway Station. They had a good time there, and left the bar after the last round.

Three white men across the street had started to chant: "Chink, chink, fucking chink".

'Chink' is an ethnic slur for Chinese equivalent to 'wop' for Italians, 'kike' for Jews, 'mick' for Irish, etc. During the fall of the Qing Dynasty, many Chinese were forced to leave their motherland because of poverty and they sought employment in foreign countries. Many were sold as indentured laborers. They were often regarded as sub-human. (Nevertheless, Chinese contributed to the development of the western part of the United States. In Europe, during the First World War, Chinese laborers built the railroads that allowed the Allies to defeat Germany and the Central Powers.) In the Australia of the 1950s – and in other English-speaking countries for that matter – there were few Chinese students studying or working abroad who were not objects of verbal abuse.

Jeffrey, a good friend of Duncan's, had also studied *Wing Chun* with Yip Man before he left Hong Kong. He was big and muscular, and was acknowledged as the leader and protector of his mates. But, with a few drinks under his belt, he was also less cautious and restrained. Taking into consideration their superiority in number, he walked across the street toward the group.

"Stop calling us chink, you bastards."

"Chink, chink, fucking chink." They had also had a few drinks, chanting away with abandon.

"One more word and I will beat the shit out of you."

This challenge sobered them up. One of them, ready to step forward, looked Jeffrey in the eyes and said: "Fuck you. You want to fight?"

"Any time." Jeffrey was confident.

"One against one. Only you and me."

"OK."

They went into a lane leading to an open area at the back. The white man, taller than Jeffrey, looked tough and muscular. He raised his arms and was ready to fight.

It was *Wing Chun* against boxing. It didn't take long to see who dominated the bout, and it wasn't Jeffrey. The man was fast, and his punches were heavy. Jeffrey tried to kick him but he failed to make an impression.

His opponent punched and hooked, and he got Jeffrey in the head and stomach. Jeffrey was not good enough to cause any damage with his chain punches. He was knocked to the ground unconscious, his jaw broken and split in the center.

"Every chink must leave St. Mary's by Wednesday. And if I see any of you again, I will beat the shit out of every one of you," the winner declared.

They discovered later that he was a boxing instructor.

An ambulance was called, and Jeffrey was transferred to the hospital. He suffered from black eyes, a bleeding nose and a broken jaw that had to be wired. Worse, there were bone chips on his skull. He was in the hospital for two weeks.

On their way up the steps of the bridge across the railway tracks, Duncan's friends saw a white man with three young ladies approaching. It was immediately pointed out to Duncan that this was the guy! What a coincidence!

It was an impasse. He recognized the group.

"Get out of my way, chink."

Duncan stopped in front of him and looked into his eyes. For several tense moments, the two pugilists stared at each other.

"Is it true that you said you wanted us to leave St. Mary's by Wednesday?"

"Yes, I want all of you to leave. If I see any of you still here by then, I will beat the hell out of every one of you."

"I tell you what. If you want to beat us, you don't have to wait till Wednesday. Beat me now."

"Do you want to fight like your pal in the hospital?" Still, there was a trace of hesitation in his manner.

"Oh yes."

"Come back next Wednesday night."

"It would be impolite to make you wait. Let's fight now."

The Australian was surprised. He had seriously injured a much larger person the night before, and this small guy was ready and eager to fight on the spot. Something wasn't right. His intuitive alarm bells were ringing.

"Can't you see I'm busy? Come back next Wednesday night."

"Fight, or get out of my way!"

With three beautiful young ladies beside him, the Australian had no way to back off.

"Out in the open then – only you and me." He was alone and figured that they might gang up on him. He pointed to an open space below and beyond the bridge.

Accompanied by his girlfriends, he walked down the bridge to the open space. Duncan followed him. The rest of the Chinese group remained and watched from the bridge. It was Sunday and still early. There were hardly any commuters about.

Duncan's confidence rattled the Australian, who started to set the rules: "No open hands, no chops and no kicks. No punches below the belt either."

"OK," Duncan assented.

The two men faced off. As Duncan moved to remove his jacket, the other man launched a hard right arm punch. Taken off guard, Duncan could merely duck, and the punch landed painfully on his right shoulder. Instantly, Duncan swept his right leg at him.

"No kicks," he stopped Duncan, who withdrew his leg in mid-air, threw off his jacket and started to fight.

The clearing was uneven and scattered with pebbles. It was more difficult shifting his feet than on level ground.

The Australian weighed over 200 pounds and was half a head taller than Duncan. He was cautious. Like a seasoned fighter, he always moved backward after he jabbed or punched. He avoided giving Duncan the opportunity to *stick* his arms. He moved left, he moved right, testing Duncan's reaction. Duncan followed his movements, facing him all the time, and shifted toward him gradually. The Australian was more or less circling him. His tactic was hit and run. With his longer arms and legs, and the uneven ground, it was difficult for Duncan to hit him. His right shoulder was still too painful to raise his arm above shoulder level. The Australian was hitting while Duncan *covered*. Duncan's weakened punches were not hurting him. The only thing was to wait for him to charge so that the *Wing Chun collision* could hurt him. For this reason, the fight lasted much longer than it normally would. Luckily, none of the boxing instructor's punches landed solidly on Duncan's body, or he would have been finished.

Suddenly, the Australian feinted a left punch, charging at Duncan while swinging a mean right hook. Duncan *covered* his right fist with his left palm while turning his horse forward to the right. Simultaneously, he threw a straight punch with his right fist, which landed squarely on his jaw. Duncan immediately followed with the *chase*, and his opponent fell backward, landing on the ground. As he fell, he pulled Duncan with him. Duncan fell on top of him and locked his head with his right arm. The Australian wrapped his left arm round Duncan's neck and tried to free himself by pushing with his right hand. Duncan screwed his left thumb on his opponent's right cheek, causing so much pain that he had to release his grip on Duncan's neck.

Duncan speaking: *Had I learned the killing techniques from the mysterious old man (see Chapter 4) before then, I could have easily flipped him over, and there was nothing he could have done about it.*

The girls were screaming.

After struggling awhile, the two fighters agreed to free each other. Duncan got up first, watching his opponent, who was still on his knees, trying to get up. The Australian was now really mad, and this made him irrational. As a last resort, he charged at Duncan, trying to grab his waist. In this, he succeeded, but Duncan punched him so hard on the left side of his forehead that he heard bone crack. Duncan broke his own right second and third knuckles.

For a brief moment, the instructor was unconscious. When he got up, he gave Duncan his hand and remarked that it was a good fight.

Duncan picked up his jacket and left the scene. He rejoined his friends who heaped lavish praise upon him. Then they went to visit Jeffrey in the hospital.

Later they learned that the instructor had been admitted to the hospital with concussion and a cracked skull.

Subsequently, Duncan was arrested for fighting because his opponent required hospitalization, and he was locked up for a night. Released the next day, no charges were brought against him. After all, it was a fair fight.

Duncan Leung vs. boxing instructor

The instructor struck
Leung's right shoulder

Leung threw off his jacket...

...*covered* the right punch,
and hit the instructor's jaw

Chapter 22

CHOPSTICKS

Sydney
1961

Perfect practice produces extraordinary skills
孰 能 生 巧
(*shu neng sheng qiao*)
Ouyang Xiu (歐陽修, 1007-1072)

Ouyang Xiu was one of the *Eight Prose Masters of the Tang-Song Period* (唐宋八大家; Tang Dynasty 618-907 and Song Dynasty 960-1279). He employed the following story to indicate that skills are ultimately dependent upon practice. If one's practice can be made perfect, the result is invariably an extraordinary level of skill. Needless to say, this is easier said than done.

An archer who was the best in his day was naturally proud of his talent. One day, he was aware of an old man watching him practice and he also noticed the old man was not too impressed when he shot the bull's eye nine times out of ten. This lack of respect for his skill, acknowledged far and wide, upset him and he could not help but ask the old man the reason why. The old man, an oil seller by trade, told him it was just a matter of practice and there was nothing extraordinary about it. He then demonstrated to the archer that he, himself, could pour oil right through the tiny center hole of a Chinese coin without spilling a drop on the metal. The archer was impressed and appreciated the old man's reasoning.

In the early 1960s, Sydney's Chinatown consisted of just a couple of streets. There were Chinese restaurants, shops selling various goods and produce, as well as the ubiquitous gambling dens. As in Chinatowns throughout the world, proprietors were expected to pay protection money to the triads if they expected to stay in business. The various triads carved Chinatown into spheres of interest, and each gang ruled in their particular territories. They each managed their operation and collected their income. It was peaceful and everybody was at ease, if not exactly happy, with this state of affairs. Pool halls, more elegantly known as billiard parlours, were located on the fringes of Chinatown and most of them were run by the Thais. Thai martial artists are well known for their fierce fighting styles and vicious kicks. It wasn't wise to stir up trouble there.

Duncan's friends decided he needed to learn how to shoot pool, so one day they went to a billiard parlour. The joint was crowded and filled with smoke. There were half a dozen tables and all were occupied. One of Duncan's party went over to book a table. Duncan and his three friends milled around the tables, watching and waiting for their turn.

Duncan was sitting on a bench against the wall, holding a bowl of steaming *wonton* noodles in one hand and a pair of chopsticks in the other. Every time one of the players wanted to pot, he had to move out of the way. Invariably people bumped into one another, setting off many unnecessary arguments and fights.

"Get out of my way. Are you blind?" a player shouted at one of Duncan's friends who was standing near the table. He was no doubt too slow for the player's taste because he poked his cue into the friend's stomach. Duncan, who was sitting just behind the player, reacted by kicking his rear end, sending him tumbling forward. He balanced himself and turned round, staring at Duncan. The player was Chinese. One thing led to another – cursing and pushing – and finally a free-for-all fight. Duncan's friends did not know how to fight and they were trying desperately to find their way out. Duncan stayed behind to cover their exit.

Then the Thai bouncers came – seven or eight of them. One of them punched at Duncan, who reacted quickly and threw the hot bowl of soup at him. Another Thai charged him with a cue. Duncan *covered* and simultaneously lashed out with a wicked kick, which unfortunately missed. The Thai was swinging the cue in the air as if it were a long pole. The cue broke on something, splintered, and the bouncer pointed the sharp end at Duncan like a knife. Duncan, still holding his chopsticks, squared off.

The Thai bouncer held the sharp-edged cue like a spear and he looked like he knew what he was doing. Duncan positioned the chopsticks as if they were a pair of *Eight-Chop Knives*. When the bouncer poked at him, Duncan shifted his horse to the right and *covered*. The very moment he caught the advancing cue between the chopsticks, Duncan immediately shifted his right foot forward, while simultaneously poking the right chopstick into the bouncer's face. He followed up with the left chopstick to the same target. Screaming in pain, the bouncer dropped his cue and covered his bloody face with both hands.

The rest of the Thais stopped and ran over to help him. This gave Duncan the opportunity to escape. He jumped on a billiard table and ran from table to table until reaching the front door. He darted out quickly and raced up the street, never to return.

AMERICA, HERE I COME

In 1973 a star fell in the East. Bruce Lee died in his prime under mysterious circumstances. The news stunned people – not just martial arts and movie fans – worldwide. An estimated million people lined the route of his funeral procession. What a waste in so many ways.

It is said that *fortune never arrives in pairs and misfortune never walks alone* (福無重至禍不單行 *fu wu chong zhi huo bu dan xing*). If you have a good run at the casino one day, you should not press your luck by going the next day. Conversely, if you have a bad run at a casino one day, avoid going the next day because misfortune tends to come more than once. This Chinese folk wisdom has wide application in life. Thank heaven for your luck and do not get greedy for more than your allotted share; thank heaven also that you were unlucky only once. Remember this idiom, and it will save you money and aggravation.

In 1973 the Hong Kong Stock Market, trading with an average P/E of 110, crumbled. The local Hang Seng Index plunged from its historical high of 1,780 to 158. Just like the 1929 Wall Street Crash in the USA, billions of dollars of paper wealth evaporated overnight. Recession was worldwide and depression ensued in Hong Kong. Shareholders who had made fortunes during the bull-runs could not resist the temptation to buy more when the market was on the way down, when they should have taken profit and run.

When they got their first taste of the bear market and could see that their fortune was gradually nibbled away, instead of cutting losses, they waited for their luck to change until the bears gobbled them up. There were people going bankrupt and there were people going crazy. The only institutions doing good business were psychiatric hospitals. Otherwise, business was poor in every sector.

Who would buy cars when many car owners were trying to unload theirs, together with their real estate as well, just to raise cash? At the time, Duncan was in the car business. In addition, he had invested heavily in stocks.

Out of the blue came an opportunity. Stephen, the friend Duncan had rescued from the triad dragon head in Taipei in 1968, called to ask if he would go to New York to find buyers for sheepskin jackets. In the wake of the '73 crash and subsequent worldwide recession, buyers would not come to the Far East. Sellers had to go to the West. Duncan spoke English. Stephen offered him a good deal including all expenses. He had nothing better to do at the time and accepted the offer gratefully.

A short trip – to last no longer than a month – was planned. The idea was to troll for customers for three weeks and then go to Toronto to pick up Duncan's wife Amy, who was visiting relatives, before returning to Hong Kong.

Chapter 23

First Fight in the U.S.

New York
1974

First time away from thatched cottage
初 出 茅 廬
(*chu chu mao lu*)
Romance of the Three Kingdoms (三國演義)
Luo Guan-zhong (羅貫中)

Liu Bei (劉備 161-223), the King of Shu during the Three Kingdoms
Period (220-265), humbly paid Kong Ming (孔明 181-234), the
legendary military strategist, three visits at his thatched cottage to
invite him to be his military counselor. Against overwhelming odds
Kong Ming defeated Cao Cao (曹操 155-220) in his debut battle
when he was still only in his twenties. It was recorded as the first
triumph away from the thatched cottage.

D uncan arrived in New York City right after the New Year.
There was a Chinese restaurant on Delancy Street, then
just on the fringe of Chinatown. He was introduced to the owner,
Henry Leung (no relation), and hung out almost nightly and on
weekends. Duncan was not doing well as a salesman of sheepskin
coats. After two months of pounding the pavements, he had not

gotten a single order.

Delancy Street, formerly a cornerstone of the Jewish Lower East Side, was a less than desirable neighborhood. It was populated by prostitutes and pimps, many of whom dined at Henry's. Even their business was suffering.

One evening, business at the restaurant was very slow. Henry, busy talking to somebody, asked Duncan to deliver a couple of dishes to a table. He took the dishes from the kitchen and walked up the aisle. He saw a huge leg sticking out on the aisle, and looked up to see a large African-American sitting alone, waiting to be served. He was at least six foot four and weighed 300 pounds, twice Duncan's size. More startlingly, he was in heavy drag, down to makeup, wig, and diamonds. He spread his legs apart and partially covered the area between his thighs with the front part of his skirt. The color of his underwear was clearly visible. He wore pumps with shoelaces tied round his calves.

"Excuse me, would you mind moving your leg. You are blocking the aisle." Duncan could not help staring.

The transvestite looked up nonchalantly and cursed. He was not going to move his leg out of the aisle and was waiting to see if Duncan would do anything about it. After delivering the dishes, Duncan returned and stepped on his outstretched right foot on purpose. When the American stood up he looked even bigger and taller. Towering over Duncan, he shoved the table away and swung his right arm.

Duncan was 32 years old, in his prime in terms of *Kung Fu* practice and combat experience. His body reacted without thought.

Duncan *covered* (slapped, to be exact) the outstretched right forearm with his left hand, steering his right arm and body toward Duncan to his right, and punched the transvestite in the nose, the weakest spot on the face, with his right fist. He was stunned and blood was dripping from his nostrils. He fell back on the chair, crushing it and landing with a crash on the floor. Getting up, he vainly tried to swing at Duncan with the other arm. He grabbed Duncan and pulled him in. Both fell, but Duncan was on top of him. A few more punches and the rambunctious transvestite was unconscious.

Everything happened so fast. Now sirens were rapidly approaching, and Henry told Duncan to beat it; he would handle the rest. Duncan vanished into the night, not daring to return to the restaurant for some time.

The victim was carried to the hospital by an ambulance. Henry was arrested and taken into custody because he was the owner. He refused to reveal Duncan's identity or whereabouts and ended up spending two nights in the precinct jail cell, an excruciatingly painful experience he would rather forget.

Henry had not known Duncan practiced *Kung Fu*. He was curious and fascinated. They became good friends, and there would come a day when Duncan was able to return Henry's favor.

Chapter 24

First Shots

New York
1974

A bolt from the blue
一 鳴 驚 人
(*yi ming jing ren*)
Han Feizi (韓非子, 280-233 B.C.)

Han Feizi composed a well known fable about an unusual bird which generally kept quiet and maintained a low profile, and so went unnoticed until it amazed people with its loud, shrill crow. Similarly, it was not yet time for a talented *Kung Fu* artist to showcase his ability, which would someday amaze the martial arts world.

Henry's restaurant had the usual large glass front facing the street. Entering through the foyer, there was also a glass door and a glass partition.

The restaurant itself was rectangular and deep with two rows of tables all the way to the kitchen at the back. There was a staircase, midway down the restaurant opposite the counter, leading to the basement with its door facing the kitchen. The two tables between the door and the kitchen could not be seen from the street and they were some customers' favorites.

One night quite late, at nearly 2 a.m., there were two gangs occupying a few tables at the back of the restaurant. One group was Puerto Rican, and the other was Dominican. Sitting at one of the favorite tables were two Caucasians eating a late supper. Several tables at the front were also occupied. Duncan was sitting by himself on a bar stool, sipping coffee and chatting with Henry.

Suddenly, yells and curses in Spanish were heard from the rear. To Duncan, it was *West Side Story* revisited – the Sharks and the Jets! Switchblades were opened. Tables and chairs were pushed out of the way. Two gang members, one from each group, moved into the middle and started circling one another. A fight was imminent.

Surprisingly, the two Caucasians sitting at their table appeared unruffled by all the commotion. They remained seated and watched like spectators at a stage play.

The fight made no sense to Duncan. Instead of moving in at one another, they were pacing the floor to the right and to the left, staring at each other. One guy wielded a knife with a ten-inch blade, and he made the first move. He lunged forward, trying to stab his opponent's stomach. His opponent, a smaller guy with a switchblade about six inches long, dodged backward.

Neither of them was particularly adept with a knife in Duncan's professional opinion. There was no technique, no finesse. They were simply jabbing and slashing, ducking and dodging, like two animals fighting for the same turf.

So far there was no contact, but the smaller guy was losing ground and he was almost cornered. Finally, his nerve crumbled. He made a dash for the door. His opponent slashed, but he ducked to avoid being cut. A second slash caught him on the back, however. The wound was long and deep. Nevertheless, he did not fall and continued to run for the door. As he scurried out, he knocked over chairs and tables in an attempt to delay his pursuer.

Duncan was still sitting on the stool when the smaller one ran past him. But his pursuer was not giving up. Holding his knife, he chased after his quarry. When he was about to pass, Duncan's instinct kicked in.

Wordlessly, Duncan grabbed his right hand and turned it outward, then inward so that his wrist and right elbow were forced to follow, and twisted inward with the tip of the blade pressing against his throat. Simultaneously he grabbed his left wrist and bent it backward so that his left arm was twisted behind his back. He was locked in a position with his head stuck between Duncan's upper arm and chest, like an ostrich. With the tip of his knife still in Duncan's right grip, pressing against his throat, he was very much under control.

Duncan ordered the gang members to get out, and they exited, quietly filing past. After they had all left the restaurant, Duncan accompanied the guy to the door with the blade still pressing against him. Retaining the knife, he gave him a shove through the front door and out onto the street. Duncan tossed the knife into the street behind him, and watched as he ran away.

As Duncan reentered the restaurant, glass suddenly shattered all around him. At first he thought some of the gang members were throwing stones at the restaurant windows. But as he turned around he saw a man aiming a handgun at him from only six feet away! He was stunned and momentarily froze on the spot, facing the terrible marksman who missed two more shots before Duncan could even move.

Duncan dashed back inside and jumped behind the counter. Meanwhile, there was chaos in the restaurant. People were screaming and ducking under tables. When there were no more shots, Duncan stood up. Before long, officers of the New York City Police Department arrived. The two Caucasians sitting at the favorite table got up and approached the counter.

One of them said: "We saw what happened. You are very good. You seemed to know what you were doing. Are you staying here?"

"No, I just came. I am visiting my friend."

"Do you come here often?"

"I come here all the time."

It turned out they were plain-clothes cops, and they left with the rest of the policemen.

Two days later, they came back to Henry's.

"Do you know *karate* or some kind of *Kung Fu?*" one guy asked.

"Yes, Chinese *Kung Fu.*"

"Do you have a school here?"

"No, I am just visiting," Duncan replied.

"Why don't you open a school and we will come to learn from you." They seemed very sincere.

"I can't stay in the United States. I have no green card."

"That's no problem. We can take care of the green card if you agree to stay."

Duncan called his wife who was visiting relatives in Toronto and told her what had happened, and she agreed to the new plan. He picked her up in Canada and returned to New York City. It would be their home for the next two years.

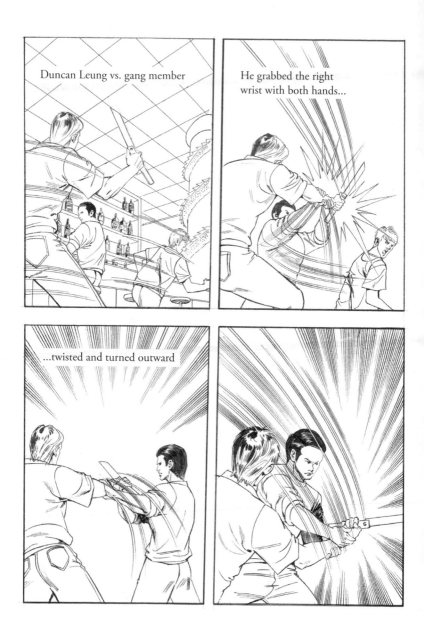

Duncan Leung vs. gang member

He grabbed the right wrist with both hands...

...twisted and turned outward

Chapter 25

First Disciple

New York
1974

Learn and then know you don't know
Teach and then know you don't understand
學 然 後 知 不 足 教 然 後 知 困
(*xue ran hou zhi bu zu jiao ran hou zhi kun*)
The Book Of Rites
Confucius

"The more you learn, the more you realize you don't know" is another way of expressing this wisdom from Confucius, who also pointed out that "Teaching benefits students and teachers alike (教學相長 *jiao xue xiang zhang*)."

Teaching is particularly difficult because in order to properly instruct, one must possess a keen insight into the actual level of the student and convey knowledge in a manner that he can understand. Only a cruel or incompetent teacher blames his charge instead of taking responsibility for the student's failure.

Because Duncan did not even have a job, his criteria for renting a studio to teach *Kung Fu* were that it had to be big and the rent had to be affordable. He found the perfect site, a 2000 square foot space in a two-story building on Great Jones Street. The rent was only $300 a month. However, because Duncan's knowledge of New York was minimal, it wasn't until later that he figured out it was located in one of the least desirable neighborhoods in the city.

He placed an advertisement in a local Chinese newspaper and hung out his shingle. At the time, there were many martial arts and *Kung Fu* studios in New York's Chinatown, teaching a variety of systems and styles, including – thanks to the popularity of Bruce Lee – *Wing Chun*.

It was a great time to be a *Kung Fu* instructor because there were plenty of students to go around. Every instructor proclaimed his system's superiority over all others and every instructor claimed his version of the system was purer and more authentic than his competitors. Meanwhile, the public had an almost impossible task separating truth from hype.

For an instructor new in town such as Duncan, with no local connection or affiliation, it was interesting. Challengers abounded from every system, including his own, who were anxious to test his mettle and show up the newcomer.

Before Duncan's studio was ready for occupancy, he used Henry's Chinese restaurant as a correspondence address in his advertisement. The very day the advertisement appeared, someone walked into the restaurant and demanded: "Who is Leung *Sifu*?"

Henry answered: "I am. What do you want?" He thought the man was asking for the chef!

"I learned *Wing Chun* from Liang Xiang (梁相), my instructor in Hong Kong. Everything there is to learn, I have learned from him."

Henry played with him: "You must be very good. Why don't you *Chi Sau* with my younger brother?"

"O.K."

"Ah Hung, someone wants to *Chi Sau* with you."

Duncan was sitting at one of the favorite tables, reading a newspaper and having a bowl of wonton noodles, but he was delighted to meet a *Wing Chun* brother. He came over and saw a Chinese in his late twenties. The man wore a black Chinese suit with jacket buttons undone, exposing a clean white t-shirt covering an elevated chest. He wore the typical *Kung Fu* slippers, black cloth top with thin soles.

"You are Leung *Sifu*?" He was polite but arrogant.

"Yes, what can I do for you?"

"Someone told me you claim to be Yip Man's disciple." This was said with obvious skepticism since Duncan looked much younger than his actual age. It was not unusual for people to question just from a chronological point of view how he could possibly have studied *Wing Chun* with Yip Man.

"He is my *Sifu*."

"I also learned *Wing Chun*." It was evident from his facial expression that he had never heard of Duncan and didn't think much of him either.

It was not surprising. Yip Man became famous through Bruce Lee's career. He had become so well known that everyone wanted to learn *Wing Chun* from him. Also, so many of his students had emigrated to different parts of the world that he could genuinely accept the accolade 桃李滿天下 (*tao li man tian xia*), which literally means *peaches and plums reach the sky and earth*, that is, the world.

Duncan, being one of his few private disciples, had been taught at home. He had left Hong Kong for Australia in 1959 and returned to Hong Kong in 1964. Between 1964 and 1972, the year Yip Man passed away, he had only seen his *Sifu* occasionally. Therefore, not many of Yip Man's students were aware of Duncan. Those who were knew him as 'Hung *chai*' or 'Ah Hung', the name by which his *Sifu* used to call him. Nor was Duncan very familiar with the students or disciples of Yip Man who came after him.

"I would like to see your *Wing Chun*. Why don't we *Chi Sau*?" the man continued.

Duncan assented and invited him to go down to Henry's basement.

There ensued a friendly conversation in which the man told Duncan of his years of *Wing Chun* study with Duncan's *Kung Fu* elder brother, Liang Xiang, in Hong Kong, and of the man's subsequent university education in Ohio.

As previously explained, *Chi Sau* (黐手) or *sticky hand* is unique to *Wing Chun Kung Fu*. It is a practice of the 'sense of contact' and is not a fighting technique. Many *Wing Chun* practitioners erroneously think *Chi Sau* is for fighting, but in reality nobody uses *Chi Sau* in genuine combat. Using *Chi Sau* alone, one can feel the skill of a *Wing Chun* practitioner, but that's all.

When people invite each other to *Chi Sau*, it is a polite way of testing how good one is. It is different from *Jiang Shou* (講手), which is a challenge to determine who is the better fighter. That being said, *Chi Sau* often leads to *Jiang Shou*.

They stood before each other and intertwined their outstretched arms in the usual manner. Before the man even moved his arms, Duncan could sense he was not good enough. He knew for certain he could not get away from him, so Duncan allowed him to initiate the moves and just followed along. Duncan was certain the man could not even tell what he was doing.

The man became impatient and started to exert greater force

in his movements. Duncan's arms reacted accordingly. No matter how hard he tried, he could not withdraw his arms from Duncan's seemingly weak movements.

In his frustration, he threw a punch at his superior opponent – a big mistake. The cheap shot did not work, of course. Duncan dragged him toward himself, and with the advancing force of the punch, sent him sprawling ten feet across the floor. All things considered, it was still a gentle reprimand for overstepping the bounds of *Chi Sau* propriety.

The man got up and walked back to Duncan: "Your *Chi Sau* is so different. I have never seen anything like it. Let's try again."

"It is all the same. You need more practice."

"Would you fight with me?"

"No, you are not good enough."

"Let me try."

Actually, Duncan felt that the man was not that bad, his biggest mistake being that he kept disconnecting during *Chi Sau*. As mentioned earlier, *Chi Sau* is not for fighting; it is a training exercise. Once contact was broken during *Chi Sau*, an offensive situation was created, and Duncan's reflexes kicked in and it was natural to strike.

"Why don't you try this?" Duncan suggested. "I'll just stand here, and you try to hit me whatever way you like. I won't move. If you can hit me, I lose."

Duncan had maneuvered him into a real dilemma: to be invited to fight a man who would not move his feet was insulting. But to lose to a man not moving his feet was far worse.

"Don't worry. You cannot hurt me. Go ahead," Duncan encouraged him.

He could not resist and accepted Duncan's offer. He shifted his feet and charged forward, throwing a straight punch with his right fist and guarding his chest with his left palm. Duncan slapped on his outstretched right forearm with his left hand (拍手 *pak sau*), dragging him forward, and slapped his face with his right hand. It was more of a gentle push than a slap, but he bled anyway and fell backward to the ground. He got up and said nothing. They went back upstairs into the restaurant and sat down at a table.

Duncan helped him to staunch blood running down from his nose with ice and tissues. It was about three in the afternoon, and there were hardly any customers. For three hours he just sat there, lost in thought, without uttering a word. Suddenly, he fell to his knees before Duncan: "Please accept me as your disciple."

"I haven't started teaching yet and my studio is not even ready," Duncan replied mildly.

"I won't get up until you accept me."

It was just like a cliché from a Chinese *Kung Fu* movie. And just like the venerable *sifus* on film, Duncan was moved by his sincerity and agreed to accept him as his disciple.

"Don't rush. I will accept you when my studio is ready." Duncan reassured him.

But the man was impatient and would not wait. He went through the ritual of *three kneels and nine kowtows* in the basement at Henry's restaurant and became Duncan's first formal disciple. His name was Ma Man Nam (馬文南).

Chapter 26

LOCKED GATE MATCH

New York
1974-1976

Experienced through a hundred battles
身 經 百 戰
(*shen jing bai zhan*)
Zi Zhi Tong Jian (資治通鑑)
Sima Guang (司馬光, 1019-1086)

In contemporary times, the expression *experienced through a hundred battles* is often used to describe someone with vast experience in any field. Duncan tells an anecdote when someone boasts of his years of experience:

"I knew a technician who proudly told me 'I have twenty years of experience.' So I asked him: 'What do you do?' He answered: 'I turn nuts at Ford!' He called that 'experience'. He probably had one day's experience, which he repeated for twenty years. No wonder he talked like nuts. I would too if I had to do what he did, day in and day out."

Repetition is not experience. Machines have replaced much of the drudgery of former times, and this trend continues apace. Through varied experience – and personal commitment – we improve over time, gaining valuable skill and knowledge.

As a new *Kung Fu* instructor in town, Duncan faced tests by instructors from every martial arts discipline, system and style, including his own *Wing Chun* clan. Rather than come to welcome him or to offer practical advice to a fellow martial arts practitioner, they came to size him up and to issue a challenge. Wanting to show their students how good they were, these leaders invariably marched in with an air of contempt, followed by retinues of students and disciples who expected to learn real-life fighting lessons from their instructors. They were never disappointed at 3 Great Jones Street on the edge of New York's Chinatown.

Karate masters, practitioners of *Tae Kwon Do*, Western boxing, Thai Boxing and other Chinese *Kung Fu* schools and styles arrived at the doorstep almost daily. This gave Duncan the opportunity to test his skills against different systems and provided valuable practical experience. However, after a while, even this game became tiresome, so he designed what he called the *Locked Gate Match* as a deterrent.

In the *Locked Gate Match,* the winner got the keys. To get out, the challenger had to beat Duncan and take the keys away. There would be only one way out – the winner would walk away, and the loser would be carried out. While students need instruction in how to fight, teachers often need to learn when *not* to fight. This was the lesson taught at 3 Great Jones Street. Various challenging leaders, *Sifus*, and teachers proudly strode in and were promptly carried out.

Duncan himself received an education. Facing challengers continuously for months, he also learned. He was hit and injured, but he knew he had to beat them or leave town.

The *Locked Gate Match* did achieve its objective, but only to a certain extent. Those who wished to come for free lessons would have second thoughts. The river of challengers finally slowed to a trickle. But there were always nuts who – in Duncan's phrasing – were destined to meet their nutcracker.

Duncan showed his resourcefulness, confidence and courage. He went to visit every martial arts school in New York City instead, and offered himself up for challenge.

Chapter 27

OH, CAROL!

New York
1975

Woman with a hero's virtues
巾幗鬚眉
(*jin guo xu mei*)
Nei Hai Hua (孽海花)
Zeng Po (曾朴, 1872-1935)

Zeng Po, author of *Nei Hai Hua*, used *Jin guo xu mei* (巾幗鬚眉) as a description for a heroic woman having the virtues expected of a heroic man. In ancient China, *Jin guo* (巾幗) referred to female headgear, and this term was also used to address a woman. *Xu mei* (鬚眉) meaning *bears and eyebrows* was an equivalent alternative way to address a man. *Jin guo sheng xu mei* (巾幗勝鬚眉), meaning woman better than man, is not uncommon these days.

Over two centuries ago, English writers Mary Wollstonecraft (1759-1797), author of *Vindication of the Right of Women*, and her daughter Mary Wollstonecraft Shelley (1797-1851), author of the famous novel *Frankenstein*, vigorously advocated equal rights using their literary talent.

Around the same time, during the reigns of Emperors Qianlong (1736-1795), Jia Qing (1796-1820) and Dao Guang (1821-1850), a nun by the name of Wu Mei and her disciple Yim Wing-chun introduced a revolutionary system of *Kung Fu* in China, inventing an unsurpassed style. They used martial arts to fight for justice for their gender in the East, just as the mother and daughter above used pens in the West.

Wing Chun Kung Fu was the latest and greatest invention in martial arts. Its basic movements are to fighting like numbers are to mathematics, notes to music, the letters of the alphabet to languages, the elements to physics. In theory, there is no limit to the number of fighting techniques that can be created from the basic movements of *Wing Chun*. How ironic that a woman should contribute such a system to a field that had been dominated by men for thousands of years.

The fight for equal rights has consistently progressed in the West, though more slowly in the East. Today there are men who envy the success of many women, and there are also men who wish they could master the fighting techniques of a revolutionary system founded by women.

Wing Chun, founded by women and named after a woman, was designed to beat men. Man, a conceited creature, should not be scornful of a woman when she steps into the ring. To the contrary, he should pay more attention.

One day, four young Chinese males walked into Duncan's studio while many of the students were practicing. Looking around, Duncan assumed they were interested in the *Wing Chun* system.

"I would like to see what your *Wing Chun* is like," one young man in his twenties stated.

"Sure, you are welcome to watch."

"No, we want to spar with your students."

Knowing they were looking for a little action, Duncan replied: "No problem. We like friendly sparring."

The one who looked like the leader of the pack pointed at two of Duncan's students – the American twins Joe and Gary Young – and said: "Can I spar with them?" They were the biggest and beefiest of Duncan's students.

"I don't think so. They are twice your size. They could kill you. I don't want anyone to get hurt." Duncan was not joking.

A demure voice spoke up: "*Sifu,* can I try? I have not done any sparring before." It was a female student, Carol, who was volunteering.

"Why not? You have to start somewhere."

Carol was a homegrown American beauty in her early twenties, about five-foot-four. Her short blonde hair and bright blue eyes matched her lovely face – no doubt Yim Wing Chun, the Grandmaster of the First Generation, would have been proud to have such a beautiful descendant. Although she had been Duncan's student for a year, she had never fought before. But she was eager to prove herself.

The leader was not too keen to spar with Carol. Duncan promised him if he could beat her he could spar with anyone he liked. Assuming the combative stance easily recognized as *Northern Praying Mantis* (北螳螂), he prepared to dispatch this mere girl of whom he made no attempt to hide his disdain. Carol waited for the Mantis to make the first move.

The Mantis just stood there as if he were hypnotized, probably captivated by Carol's stunning appearance. Carol inched forward carefully with her arms in front of her. Duncan realized the Mantis also had no fighting experience or he would not have let Carol get so close to him. Carol attacked very fast, taking the Mantis by surprise. Suddenly, she threw a straight punch to his face, landing on his nose. The Mantis was stunned. He tried to regain his composure, but she gave him no opportunity. She *chased* and followed up with chain punches and kicks. He was on the floor in seconds. It was over so quickly.

Blood was oozing from his nose and lips. Seeing the damage she had inflicted, Carol was terrified and started to cry. They helped the Mantis get up, took him to the washroom to clean his face, and applied pressure to stop the bleeding. His black eye wasn't too bad.

When they were leaving, Duncan thought he heard someone humming a line from the Paul Anka tune: *Oh Carol, I am but a fool…*

Chapter 28

Wing Chun Woodpecker

New York
1976

No class distinction in education
有 教 無 類
(*you jiao wu lei*)
The Analects of Confucius
Confucius

Duncan believes that everybody is teachable, not just in martial arts, but academically also. A good and open teacher should be able to teach every willing individual. Methods and techniques may vary or require adaptation, but the teacher is responsible for the student's success or failure, as long as the student sincerely wants to learn.

Unfortunately our educational system is not geared for individual instruction. Failure is invariably attributed to the student, who is too slow, too lazy, or does not pay attention. Students are expected, and conditioned, to fit into the system whether it is appropriate for them or not. Taking the opposite approach, Duncan Leung adapts the teaching to fit the *Kung Fu* student. Here is a story about one such student, told in Duncan's own words.

Ralph, a Dominican in his late twenties, was a chef. He loved learning *Wing Chun*. He was powerful, determined, willing to work hard and capable of withstanding a lot of pain. But Ralph's coordination was so bad that I had to tailor-make a program especially for him.

Even after a year studying under me, Ralph wasn't ready for *bui tze* (標指), the third form of *Wing Chun*, which is considered rather difficult. However, his wrists were very strong and his fingers were like baby bananas. I told him to improve himself physically so that his power could compensate for his lack of technique. Eventually, he was able to take instruction in *bui tze*, and I found something in this form which suited him nicely. He worked hard at it and his time to shine was not far away.

Around this time, we were invited, along with other martial artists, to give a demonstration at a university in New Jersey. Typically, *Wing Chun* demonstrations tend to be boring and monotonous to watch. *Chi sau* – with and without blindfolds – is simply not a scintillating exercise to behold.

Karate, on the other hand, gets people's attention. Punching, kicking and breaking wooden boards easily arouses the interest of spectators.

A *karate* practitioner was holding a wooden board firmly between outstretched hands. His front leg bent at the knee at about ninety degrees, and his hind leg remained straight to prop up his body. As if it wasn't enough support, two more assistants propped themselves against his shoulders, one on each side. Standing in front of the wooden board in a combative stance, the demonstrator threw a straight punch or a side kick to break it in half, to vigorous applause from the crowd. Audience members were invited to try, with predictable results. A couple of big guys slammed their fists against the boards. Having no previous training, they held their hands in pain.

Then Ralph spoke up: "*Sifu*, can I try?" He sure was game.

All I could say was: "Make sure you go all the way through without holding back. If you don't break the board, you will break your fingers."

Ralph was about five foot ten, weighing 190lbs, and strong and solid. But, standing on stage, he seemed tiny beside the other volunteers.

"How would you like us to hold the board for you?" an assistant asked.

"That's OK. I'll hold it for myself," Ralph answered.

"How are you going to break it, with your head?" another *karate* person joked.

"Let me show you."

Ralph picked up a square board from the pile and grasped one side with his right palm so that the back of his hand faced upward. He extended his right arm all the way in front of him so that the board was perpendicular to the floor. Instead of punching it with his left fist, he opened his fist and fully extended his fingers so that the tips of them (the middle finger arching at the proximal inter-phalangeal joint so that the tips of the index, middle and ring fingers were level) were vertical to the board, and the edge of his palm was facing the floor. You get the picture?

With fingers fully extended, Ralph withdrew his left forearm until his hand was near his chest. He was ready. Suddenly, his hand shot out like a snake: BANG!

Not only was the board broken in half without being propped up, but he had done it *with his fingers*! Ralph made it look easy, but the *karate* people were very embarrassed. The audience laughed and thought the boards had been tampered with. They had never seen a demonstration like this before.

Meanwhile, Ralph was having a field day. He picked up another board and then another and another. Ralph didn't stop until all the boards were destroyed.

Incredible feats!

PART SIX
1976-1978

VIRGINIA

In early 1976, about a year and a half after the opening of the Great Jones Street studio, Duncan had considered returning to Hong Kong. The neighborhood around the studio where he lived was one of the worst in New York City. It was not a neighborhood in which to raise his children, especially when Ted, his eldest son, was approaching school age. The crime rate was very high. The Leung family was exposed to the less savory side of the Big Apple. Duncan and his wife seriously discussed going home when the lease expired. Then, one day, Duncan received a telephone call from Virginia Beach.

"May I speak with Duncan Leung?"

"I am Duncan Leung. Who are you?"

"I am a fire investigator calling from Virginia Beach."

"What can I do for you?"

"We would like to invite you and your family to visit Virginia Beach. We'll send you the tickets and take care of all the expenses."

"Why?"

"A group of us are looking for an instructor to teach *Kung Fu* here. We've heard a lot about you, and we're wondering if you would be interested in helping us out."

"Surely, there must be some other instructors teaching martial arts there."

"We're not looking for an ordinary instructor. We're looking for a *Wing Chun* instructor."

Duncan, who hadn't the faintest idea where Virginia Beach was, replied: "Sorry, I am not interested."

Duncan mentioned the telephone call to his wife, who pointed out that there would have been no harm in going there and taking a look around. Several days later, the fire inspector called again, asking whether he would reconsider their offer. This time, Duncan accepted. A week later, the couple and their two sons, Ted and Darren, were on the plane to Virginia Beach, once a sleepy seasonal resort town, now part of the thriving Hampton Roads region of Virginia.

They were met at the airport by David Meadows and Dr. John Newton, a local dentist with an interest in *Wing Chun*. They were given a grand tour of the city and made to feel extremely welcome. Whereas shooting incidents were frequent in their neighborhood in New York City, the Leungs found Virginia Beach – situated on the Atlantic Ocean – beautiful, clean, and free of crime. It seemed a conducive place in which to raise and educate their children. In addition, the business arrangement was enticing: it was proposed to open a school for Duncan to teach *Wing Chun* with salary and overhead guaranteed.

Duncan decided to push the envelope: "Would you hire a car for me?"

"Sure. No problem."

"I would like to have one of my students here to help me in the beginning. I will need an assistant for demonstrations."

"We will pay him too."

"One more thing."

"What is it?"

"I would like you to invite local martial arts practitioners to spar with us. Friendly sparring."

"Terrific!" They were excited.

Although Duncan was making more money in New York, the freedom afforded by the proposed arrangement was appealing. *Wing Chun* was not Duncan's career. Having been in various businesses for years, he taught *Wing Chun* to pass on the art form. Duncan accepted the offer, returned to New York only long enough to close down 3 Great Jones Street, and moved to Virginia Beach.

A friendly sparring session was set up at the local dance hall in Virginia Beach, and six or seven martial arts instructors and their followers turned up. They represented various systems of martial arts, including *Tae Kwon Do, Karate* and *Kung Fu*. (At that time, movie star Chuck Norris had two large martial arts studios in Virginia Beach, and he was also invited. Norris declined – for obvious reasons. If he won, it wouldn't prove anything, and if he lost, it would reflect poorly on him.) The atmosphere was quite friendly. After four or five sparring bouts, everybody was happy and when they parted, the mood was pleasant.

Still, just as in New York, challengers arrived at the new *Wing Chun* studio to test the new kid on the block. They were surprised first at the apparent youthfulness of *Sifu* Leung, then at the summary manner in which he disposed of all comers.

Chapter 29

The Bear

Virginia Beach
1976

Zhuge Liang outmaneuvered Zhou Yu three times
諸 葛 亮 三 氣 周 瑜
(*Zhuge Liang san qi Zhou Yu*)
Romance of the Three Kingdoms
Luo Guan-zhong (羅貫中)

Zhuge Liang (諸葛亮, 181-234), also known as Kong Ming (孔明), was a famous statesman and strategist who became a symbol of resourcefulness and wisdom. He and Zhou Yu (周瑜, 175-210), another military genius who also lived during the Three Kingdoms Period were rivals. Zhuge, though a commoner, was personally invited by King Liu Bei (劉備, 161-223) three times at his humble residence to become his military counselor and serve the Kingdom of Shu (蜀國). Zhou served the Kingdom of Wu (吳國), and was related to King Sun Quan (孫權, 182-252) by marrying the sister of the Queen.

Zhou was very jealous of Zhuge's ability and considered him a threat. Thrice he tried to eliminate Zhuge, and each time he failed when Zhuge outmaneuvered him. On the third occasion he became so frustrated and emotionally upset that he became gravely ill, an illness from which he never recovered.

His famous last words were: "Heaven! When you gave birth to Yu, why give birth to Liang (既生瑜 何生亮 *ji sheng Yu, he sheng Liang*)?" He would rather die than have another individual outshine him in the same era.

Within a week of the opening of the *Wing Chun* school, Duncan received a visit from a well-known local instructor, an African-American who taught *Tae Kwon Do*. He had learned it from a Japanese master, and was a 4th or 5th *dan* black belt in his own right. His students had won many Full Contact championships in the Commonwealth of Virginia, and he was highly respected in martial arts circles by students and instructors alike.

He arrived with nearly 20 followers of various races – Caucasian, Asian, and Black. He was polite. After introducing himself, he said he had heard a lot about *Wing Chun* and admired Bruce Lee very much. He wanted to know more about *Wing Chun*, and Duncan patiently explained its background and theory.

"What you are saying is very different from what I saw in the movies," he commented.

"What you see in the movies has little to do with *Wing Chun*. In movies, they use spectacular motion to appeal to the audience."

"I would like to see what *Wing Chun* can do against people of my size." He was getting closer to the challenge.

"That is not too difficult," said Duncan.

"I find it hard to believe. People call me the Bear."

"The only way to find out is to try," replied Duncan mildly.

The Bear was not very tall, only a couple of inches taller than Duncan. But he was heavy – stocky – and weighed at least 280 pounds, twice Duncan's size. His fists were huge. Each one of them must have been the size of a ripe cantaloupe.

"Why don't I show you something," Duncan suggested, "and see if you are impressed? If you are, then I will tell you a bit more about *Wing Chun*."

"Show me."

"I tell you what. You put your hands up and try to stop me. I am going to stand three steps away from you and I am going to tap your face, and you cannot stop me."

"No way! If you can stand three steps away from me and hit my face, I will sign up with you in front of my students."

"Are you ready?" asked Duncan as he stood three paces away from him.

"Yes, I am ready." The Bear spread his legs in a combative stance and raised his arms to protect his face.

"I am going to hit your right cheek. You better put up your guard and get ready."

"I'm ready." He was getting annoyed.

Duncan shifted forward and with lightning speed, tapped the Bear's right cheek. He was dumbfounded. He had no idea how it happened.

"No way! I don't believe this. How can it happen?" The Bear was jumping up and down like a kid.

"Nevertheless, I did it."

"I want to see that again."

"No, I do not think I am going to try again."

"I didn't see it clearly. I want to see it again." He was getting angry now.

"Why? We made a deal. Why try again?"

"Please, try one more time," he pleaded.

"This is the last time, and I am not going to do it again. This time I am going to count one, two, three."

"I'm ready for you." He stared at Duncan with his eyes wide open.

"Are you ready?"

"Here I come… one, two, three." Duncan tapped him once more on the same spot. He was one furious Bear.

"Let's fight. Nobody can hit me! Nobody can hit me!" The Bear was absolutely beside himself.

"No, I don't want to draw blood. You agreed to it. Can't you accept defeat?"

"No way. Unless you do it again." He was adamant.

"All right, but this time I am really going to hit you." Duncan was getting irritated.

"I am the Bear. You are not going to hurt me. Nobody can hurt the Bear!"

"Watch. This time I am going to hit you squarely on the face, on exactly the same spot. Are you ready now?"

"Yes, I'm ready." His hand was so close to his right cheek that there was hardly any space left.

With exactly the same move, Duncan hit him hard, squarely on his right cheek with his fist. The Bear was stunned. He wobbled on his feet. Dizzy from the force of Duncan's blow, he fell on his backside. The Bear's students helped him up to sit on a chair.

"Get me some money!" he shouted to his students. "I want to sign up right away! Now!" He was yelling. Pointing his finger at Duncan, he continued shouting: "He is my *Sensei*!" calling him the Japanese equivalent of *Sifu*.

The Bear actually did sign up. He learned from Duncan and continued to teach. His students were loyal to him and they won more championships.

To this day, Duncan and the Bear remain good friends. But how had Duncan managed to hit an experienced and skilled martial artist in the same spot on three successive occasions?

Duncan explained: "I was punching him with my right hand. He was blocking my right hand with his right hand. However, before I reached him I used my left *pak sau* to slap his defending hand down and my right hand was then able to tap him without obstacle. He felt the impact from my *pak sau*, not my hitting hand. It was not how fast I punched, but how fast I used *pak sau*, which he never saw. Everything happened so fast that he couldn't see what happened. Because he was surprised and confused, he could not think or digest what was really happening. Had he stayed calm and composed, I should not have been able to get him the second and third time."

"How did you know beforehand how he would respond?"

"I had fought with *Tae Kwon Do* practitioners before and I knew what they could do. He had never met an *Applied Wing Chun* practitioner, and therefore he did not know what to expect. It was *the unexpected beats the expected* (出奇制勝 *chu qi zhi sheng*). Over 2,000 years ago, in *The Art of War*, Sunzi explained that to defend, one uses typical strategy (正兵 *zheng bing*), but to win, one employs atypical strategy (奇兵 *qi bing*). It is the unexpected which outmaneuvers your enemy and triumphs in battle. Similarly, the element of surprise can help you outmaneuver your opponent and win a fight."

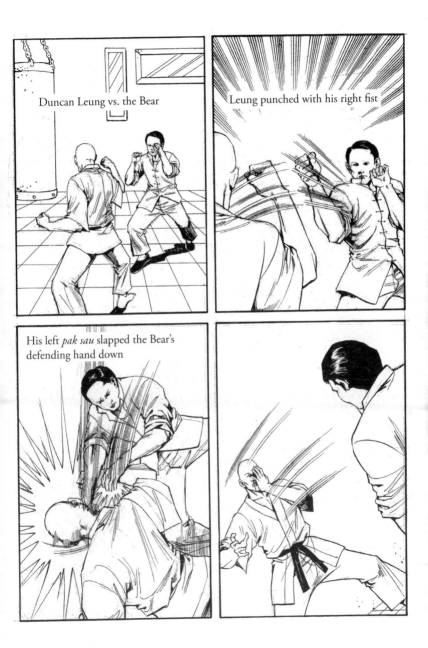

Duncan Leung vs. the Bear

Leung punched with his right fist

His left *pak sau* slapped the Bear's defending hand down

Chapter 30

President's Bodyguard

Virginia Beach
1976

Know your enemy and know yourself
Fight a hundred battles without defeat
知 彼 知 己 百 戰 不 殆
(*zhi bi zhi ji bai zhan bu dai*)
The Art of War
Sunzi

Sunzi said in *The Art of War*: "If you know what your enemy is going to do, and know your own ability, you can fight a hundred battles without defeat."

Three or four weeks after his encounter with the Bear, Duncan was teaching new students *siu nim tau* when a visitor arrived unannounced – a Korean *Tae Kwon Do* master. *Sensei* K. had many students and was esteemed in Virginia Beach. He was an inch shorter than Duncan, but was 200 pounds of solid muscle with a chest twice as thick as Duncan's. It turned out that *Sensei* K. had been a bodyguard for former President Park Chun Hee of South Korea.

He was in full *Tae Kwon Do* uniform, complete with black belt.

Behind him trailed half a dozen students. Carrying a black belt in her outstretched hands, a female American student approached Duncan deferentially.

"This is a courtesy from *Sensei* K.," she said, bowing her head as she handed Duncan the black belt.

"Thank you. Please tell *Sensei* that I will be with him in a few minutes, when I finish with my students." Duncan turned toward his visitor, nodding his head to express his appreciation.

Sensei K. nodded back. He sat on a chair, watching Duncan's students practice *siu nim tau* which, according to Duncan, is not an impressive sight. Duly unimpressed, and thoroughly bored after 15 minutes, the *sensei* arose and walked to the sandbag hanging from the ceiling. Suddenly, he punched the sandbag with his tightly clenched right fist. The punch was so hard that everyone in the room could hear the thud. It sounded as though the bag would burst.

Sensei K. took a couple of steps forward. When the pendulum came back, he turned and punched it again with his left fist, with as much force as before. He punched and kicked several more times, displaying sheer power as he vented his frustration in the presence of Duncan and the students.

"*Sensei* K., your punches are very deadly and very powerful," Duncan attempted to mollify him.

"My student gave you my courtesy." He bowed politely and introduced himself. "I am ninth *dan*. I was the bodyguard of President Park. I watch you teach *Wing Chun*. It is weak and very slow."

"They are beginners."

"I would like to see the real *Wing Chun*." Despite the fact that he had not been impressed by the drills he had witnessed, his tone and manner were quite respectful to a fellow martial arts master.

"What do you want to see?"

"Anything that will impress me."

Duncan was trying to avoid sparring with him in front of their respective students.

"Since you have such a powerful punch, do you think I can take it if you hit my body?" asked Duncan.

"I don't think so," he said.

"I would like to try. I shall stand right here. Try to punch me as hard as you can. If I move my feet, you win." This was an offer the *Sensei* could not accept as a master. But, on the other hand, he could not refuse it either. In a way, he was trapped.

"Are you sure?" He could not believe his ears, nor could anyone else present, especially after those explosive blows.

"Don't worry. You can't hurt me," said Duncan.

"Are you sure?" He was not going to let anyone question his prowess.

"Yes, just make sure you don't hold back."

In his mind, *Sensei* K. must have been wondering if Duncan was mad.

He didn't know that I was a nut before, going to studios in my teens to challenge others. But not any more. I had become a nutcracker, waiting for challengers to arrive at my studio. I knew what I was doing.

The *Sensei's* stance was typical of *Tae Kwon Do* – legs spread wide apart and fists clenched at the waist. If he feinted a kick or actually kicked, Duncan would know immediately. But he played it straight. Shifting forward, the *Sensei* punched at Duncan with his right fist as hard as he could.

Duncan snapped his advancing right forearm with his left palm in a downward move with a *pak sau* (拍手), while simultaneously punching him squarely on the forehead with enough power to send him tumbling backward to the floor. His followers helped him up.

"Very good. Very good." *Sensei* K. bowed with genuine respect, and then left.

After that incident, one of the *Sensei's* Korean students came to learn from Duncan. He remained a student of *Sensei* K. and continued to work out there. The student was rather small and was considered a weakling among his *Tae Kwon Do* peers. After six months studying with Duncan, he was able to outfight them all!

Aware of his student's remarkable improvement within such a short period of time, *Sensei* K. came to visit Duncan at his Oriental Supermarket one day.

"Duncan, can we talk in private?"

"Sure, come into the office."

"I want you to teach me *Wing Chun* privately, but I don't want anybody to know."

"That I will have to think about."

Amy, Duncan's wife, came into the office and asked what was going on. They discussed the matter and came to a decision: "*Sensei* K., I'm happy to teach you *Wing Chun*, but if you want to learn from me, it can't be a secret. Even the Bear isn't ashamed for people to know."

"I will think about it." He left. The issue was never discussed again, although Duncan and *Sensei* K. still occasionally see one another.

The real issue was the Asian preoccupation with saving face. *To want to learn is not a shame. To hide in the dark is.*

Duncan commented: "I knew exactly how the *Sensei* was going to punch. He did exactly what I asked him to do. Therefore I knew what was coming. He didn't expect someone to *cover* and punch at the same time. When you know exactly what your opponent is going to do, and also know what you yourself can do, you will win every battle and every fight. Knowing your enemy is not difficult, but knowing yourself is hard. People tend to underestimate their opponents and overrate themselves. This kind of mistake can be costly, and sometimes deadly, in a fight or in battle."

Duncan Leung vs. Korean master

The Korean punched with his right fist

Leung slapped with his left hand and punched with his right fist

Chapter 31

The Samurai

Norfolk, Virginia
1977

Rather be killed than humiliated
士 可 殺 而 不 可 辱
(*shi ke sha er bu ke ru*)
The Book of Rites (禮記)
Confucius

In ancient China, many notable individuals chose death rather than suffer humiliation at the hands of their enemies. This was also frequently the case in modern China, where during the infamous Cultural Revolution between 1967 and 1977, thousands of individuals committed suicide to escape humiliation and torture by the red guards.

Perhaps even more courageous is the individual who accepts humiliation in order to carry out a vital mission (忍辱負重 *ren ru fu zhong*).

Sima Qian (司馬遷, 145-91 B.C.), the greatest Chinese historian, was sentenced to death as a traitor on trumped-up charges. During the Han Dynasty (206 B.C. - 220 A.D.), a death sentence could be commuted either by paying a large sum of money or by suffering castration. Sima Qian had negligible wealth, but he endured the ignominy of castration for the purpose of fulfilling his father's legacy – the recording of the history of the previous two millennia. He completed *Records of the Historian* (史記 *Shi Ji*) in 91 B.C.

D uncan and his students had been invited to compete in a martial arts tournament hosted by an instructor at a local Virginia university, which gave academic credit for *Karate* classes. The following incident is related in his own words:

The in-house instructor at the university was a Japanese *samurai* who taught *Karate* to many students. He was well recognized throughout North America and in Japan. He was demanding and well known for the severity of his discipline. For example, students were whipped with a cane if they did not perform correctly, and corporal punishment was accepted as part of his training.

I do not understand how such a practice was allowed in America. After all, this wasn't Singapore. Aside from the inherent cruelty of the practice, corporal punishment is poor educational practice because fear blocks learning – no matter what the subject being taught. In this type of atmosphere, students will be afraid to ask questions for fear of punishment or ridicule. Free-flowing communication is essential to the learning process. As for martial arts, these are by no means entirely physical. Most of all, we are attempting to instill an attitude of self-confidence, something that can only arise in a trustful environment.

This was actually the first time I had watched a tournament in which competitors wear gloves and only semi-contact is allowed. Once you touch your opponent, you withdraw from contact. The person who makes first contact earns points. (Come to think of it, this is rather like the practice of certain Great Plains tribes 'counting coup' on their adversaries in battle.) While this does not work as far as actual fighting is concerned, it dose ensure that tournament participants are not injured.

Jim had studied with me for about nine months, and he was the only student of mine to enter the tournament, although a crowd of us had come to support him.

I was standing behind a panel of judges when Jim entered the ring to compete with one of the *Karate* students. The participants were reminded of the rule: no excessive force. In the first round, Jim was not awarded a single point even though he had touched his opponent many times; the explanation being that his opponent had also touched him. The judges, being unfamiliar with *Wing Chun,* did not understand that Jim was actually *covering* and counter-attacking simultaneously when it appeared as though Jim's opponent had made contact.

After the first round I asked the *samurai* why they hadn't awarded Jim points for hitting his opponent.

He answered: "Because his opponent touched him too."

"No, he did not hit Jim, but Jim clearly hit him. You made a mistake. It was a simultaneous *cover* and counter-attack. You can only see it in full contact."

Then I demonstrated the exact moves for him in slow motion.

The samurai disagreed: "No. No full contact. That is the rule."

In the second round, when Jim hit his opponent with a clear punch, he again received no point and, when I asked why, I was told:

"The way he punched had no power. It must be a full launch from the hip to score a point. He punched from a semi-cocked position with his leading arm. There's no power from that position."

"What are you talking about?" I was puzzled. Now my *Wing Chun* pride was starting to simmer.

Cocking his left fist beside his waist, the *samurai* demonstrated for me the typical *Karate* punch. "He should throw the punch from the waist. The way he threw his punch was weak and incorrect."

"I don't agree with you. The way he punched was correct and powerful."

"No, it was incorrect. *That is the rule.*" His stock phrase was really beginning to irk me.

This was going nowhere. I became furious, and finally grabbed the microphone right out of his hand. Challenging him, I shouted to the audience: "You've got to be kidding! So, you say his punch was weak and incorrect. Why don't we exchange punches? I will let you punch me first and see how powerful your punch is. I won't move my feet and I won't block. I'll just take your punch on my chest. Then, I will punch you, and see how weak and incorrect my punch is. You may not see the power, but I guarantee you will feel it."

"No, *that is the rule.*"

"Are you scared?"

"*That is the rule. That is the rule.*" He could only repeat his refrain.

In short, he refused my challenge, which was certainly not in the *samurai's* spirit.

The bout continued. Jim landed a kick on his opponent, and followed up with a left punch from a semi-cocked position. As his opponent fell backward, Jim overstretched and dislocated his left shoulder. The referee stopped the match while I went over and manipulated the dislocated shoulder back into place. I asked Jim what he wanted to do, recommending that he withdraw. Although his shoulder was very painful, Jim insisted on continuing.

He raised his left arm in front of his chest to guard, and fought with essentially one arm. The opponent, taking advantage of Jim's handicap, now charged at him like a bull, intent on delivering the *coup de grace*. Jim shifted right, avoiding the attack, and while simultaneously extending his right shoulder forward from a semi-cocked position, punched his opponent's jaw. The impact of collision was powerful because his opponent was, in effect crashing his jaw into Jim's fist. Jim's adversary crashed to the floor and the crowd erupted in applause.

Then the *samurai* stilled the crowd with the announcement that Jim had been disqualified for using excessive force.

I was appalled and protested: "His opponent was charging at him like a bull. He literally ran into my student's fist. What would you expect him to do?"

"Excessive force is against the rule."

"What about points for at least landing his punch?"

"No, he used excessive force. *That is the rule.*"

So the 'winner' was lying on the floor while the 'loser' was disqualified because he used excessive force when his opponent ran into his fist. This was martial arts turned on its head.

With respect to Duncan's unanswered challenged to the samurai, he explains how it is possible to withstand a solid punch on the chest from a *Karate* master: a *Karate* practitioner must withdraw his forearm before he punches, just like cocking the hammer of a gun before it is fired. He cannot punch with an outstretched arm. Before he punches, the distance between a target and his knuckles must be shorter than his fully extended arm, so that he can punch through. If the distance between the target and his knuckles were exactly the same as his fully extended arm, his punch would be relatively ineffective when it landed. If the distance were slightly longer, the punch would never hurt.

If you cannot reach your opponent, no matter how strong you are, your might is useless. The contrary is also true: if you can reach your opponent, even minimal power can incapacitate him. Power is derived from the stance, the twisting of the waist, and the swing of the shoulder. Distance regulates the delivery of even more power. This is the third form of *Wing Chun*.

If the *samurai* had risen to Duncan's bait and accepted the challenge, just before his punch landed, Duncan would have simultaneously sucked in his chest and swayed his torso backward to *flow with the punch* so that it would not have inflicted much damage. Duncan would have the time to do this because of the distance the punch had to travel, i.e. from the hip.

Duncan would not have exposed himself by making such an offer to an accomplished *Wing Chun* practitioner. It was Bruce Lee who publicly revealed the *inch punch* – a technique unique to *Wing Chun*. Even a master of *Karate* would not know how to use it. The *inch punch* enables one to generate power with little distance. It is dazzling to watch, and onlookers were invariably amazed when Bruce sent an opponent twice his size hurtling backwards to land ten feet away. It is accomplished by an extension of the scapula, the twisting of the hips and legs, and a strike of the wrist – the combined pushing and pulling effect of the entire upper body concentrating power into a single point. Even without cocking the arm, the combined extension elongates the reach, compensating for lack of distance. This is a core *Wing Chun* principle.

Chapter 32

BLIND SWORDSMAN

Norfolk, Virginia
1977

Bamboo in the mind
胸有成竹
(*xiong you cheng zhu*)
Su Shi (蘇軾, 1037-1101)

This epigram of Su Shi (蘇軾), one of the *Eight Prose Masters of the Tang-Song Period*, describes a person with a well thought-out plan or strategy. It comes from a poem in which he praised an artist who specialized in paintings of bamboo, and could paint them from memory without reference to an actual tree. He had internalized the essence of bamboo and could reproduce it on paper as art.

Similarly, there are martial arts practitioners who have so deeply absorbed and assimilated the techniques and methods of their particular art that, even blindfolded and unrehearsed, they can spontaneously externalize them as needed.

Being blindfolded against an opponent holding a *samurai* sword is a feat for the genius.

Chrysler Hall is Norfolk's equivalent of Madison Square Garden in New York City. Along with other local martial arts schools, Duncan had been invited to give a demonstration on stage. Ten schools in all had been invited.

Since there is nothing particularly impressive to the eye about *Wing Chun*'s forms, compared with other systems or *Kung Fu* styles, Duncan felt he had to come up with something to entertain the crowd. *Siu nim tau* and *chi sau* are boring to watch. He decided something with *Eight-Chop Knives* might prove attention-grabbing for the audience.

Duncan enlisted the Bear in the performance. He had learned how to use a *samurai* sword, although he wasn't yet an expert. For the demonstration, the Bear borrowed a genuine *samurai* sword from a friend who was an antique collector.

For the demonstration, Duncan had the Bear wear a motorcycle helmet to protect his head, hockey gloves to protect his fingers, and pads to protect his forearms, legs and stomach. Then, *Duncan was blindfolded!*

The opponents faced each other. The rules of engagement were simple: the Bear must first touch one of Duncan's knives with his sword. He could then proceed to do whatever he wanted with his sword, and Duncan would have to react.

The *samurai* sword was razor-sharp, which was apparent to the audience when the Bear tested it by chopping a wooden pole in half to impress them. Duncan's *Double Knives* were made of stainless steel. They were heavy. The blades were blunt, not sharpened. What followed was unrehearsed.

The Bear tapped Duncan's right knife with the sword, signaling he was about to attack. To Duncan, it hardly mattered what he was going to do next – chopping or slashing; his response would not vary.

The Bear knocked Duncan's lead knife (right knife) to the side with his sword, and Duncan allowed knife and hand to *flow with the motion*. Simultaneously, however, his other hand flipped the knife back up with a wrist action to slash the Bear's right forearm from underneath. (The Bear didn't feel anything because he wore a protective pad.) Anticipating the Bear's intent to raise his sword above his head to chop him in half, Duncan immediately followed by *covering* his head with the blade of his right knife facing horizontally skyward, while simultaneously flicking his left wrist to pierce. When the sword chopped heavily across the blade of his knife, Duncan's left knife had already pierced the pad protecting the Bear's stomach.

Unaware of the damage to his stomach pad, the Bear raised his sword for the second time, intending to chop again. The very moment he raised his sword, Duncan was bringing the right blade down on his helmet between his eyes, followed by the left – two sharp chops to the helmet.

Everything happened in the blink of an eye. It was over in seconds. Duncan removed his blindfold and the crowd roared.

"Duncan, what the hell have you done?" exclaimed the Bear. "You cracked my helmet and dented my friend's precious sword!"

"You should thank God that you wore a helmet, or your head could have been cracked open instead. Your sword chopped into my blade. You can't blame me."

The audience moved forward and examined the cracks in the helmet and the deeply mangled blade. But most missed the damage to the left arm pad where Duncan's slash – had this been a real fight – would have severed tendons and arteries.

In *Applied Wing Chun*, the principle is to always *cover* first. Protecting oneself from injuries is the priority. When attacking, the object is not to knock out the opponent with a single blow. Instead, one exploits the chinks in his armor, the exposed and uncovered areas. If the opponent does not know how to *cover*, he will be defenseless against your onslaught. By inflicting injuries to the uncovered areas, he is first incapacitated. The follow-up merely completes the job of finishing him off.

Short knives obviously have short reach. Against an opponent armed with a sword, one cannot initially reach his torso with short knives. But the hands and one or both forearms are accessible, depending on whether he grips his sword single- or double-handed. This illustrates another key principle of *Wing Chun*: using short weapons against a long weapon, the object is to inflict damage to the closest body part of the opponent, which would be fingers, hands, and forearms in that order. Once injury is inflicted to these areas, the rest of the body is vulnerable.

The *samurai* sword tapped Leung's right knife

Leung *covered* with the right knife and tilted the left, piercing the arm pad

He *covered* with the right knife before the sword struck...

...and pierced the stomach pad with his left knife

Chapter 33

SEAL TEAM INSTRUCTOR

Norfolk
1977

Body and mind totally convinced
心 服 口 服
(*xin fu kou fu*)
Zhuangzi (莊子, 350-286 B.C.)

One gains a person's allegiance through his heart by deeds, not with words alone, or as Zhuangzi expressed it: 心服口服 (*xin fu kou fu*).

One day, a few months after the opening of the school in Virginia Beach, a new student came to Duncan and excitedly related: "*Sifu*, a friend of mine said there is a guy called Paaaina in the Navy, who is the SEAL Team instructor."

"The U.S. Navy uses trained seals?" Duncan had never heard of the elite corps.

"He teaches members of the SEAL Team. They are the best in the Navy."

"What about him?"

"He goes around bad-mouthing *Wing Chun*, and you personally."

In those days, Duncan was still somewhat impetuous, and deeply resented any aspersions on his martial art. "I want to meet this guy and see how big a mouth he has. Where is he?"

The instructor was David Paaaina, a Hawaiian with a very tough reputation, who taught at the navy base in Norfolk. Several nights a week, he instructed the SEALs. One of Duncan's students, a sailor, offered to take him there.

However, on the night they went, Duncan was disappointed to find that Paaaina was not there. He watched the sailors work out, and finally one came over to ask what he wanted.

"I am looking for a guy named Paaaina with a big mouth."

"He's not here right now, but you can wait if you like." They decided to leave and come back the next night. Duncan found him at the navy base.

A really large Hawaiian walked up to Duncan and said: "I'm David Paaaina. I hear you are looking for me?"

"I heard you think *Wing Chun* is full of shit. I am new in town and I am teaching *Wing Chun*. I'd like to show you what shit looks like."

The instructor replied: "Not that I am afraid of you but I have never said anything bad about *Wing Chun*. This was a set up."

"What do you mean?" Duncan was puzzled.

"You don't know me, but I know you. I was at your first sparring match in Virginia Beach, although we were not introduced at the time. I am very impressed with what you can do. There is no reason for me to criticize either you or *Wing Chun*. In fact, I admire you. We have been set up. Some guys want to watch us fight, that's all."

David, as the U.S. Navy Chief SEAL Instructor, specialized in hand-to-hand combat, and was assigned to SEAL Teams Two and

Four. He was among the instructors who had gone to Duncan's demonstration in Virginia Beach in 1976 before he and his wife had even decided to move from New York City.

"Why?"

"You know. I fight a lot. I am, you might say, notorious in Virginia. Some guys just want to see if you can beat me."

"Sure. Let's try now."

"No. I know what you can do and I have heard stories about you. I don't want to fight with you. It's not worth it."

Paaaina was younger than Duncan. Still, he cooled Duncan down.

"Why don't you show me my weaknesses?" he suggested.

"Sure."

It was a sight to watch this huge Hawaiian demonstrating the *Southern Praying Mantis* (南螳螂). Even Duncan thought he was good, and he looked like a giant mantis, hopping here and there, poking, punching and kicking. Duncan pointed out his weak spots, and showed him how he would have attacked them. Paaaina, for his part, was impressed. The discussion was very friendly indeed.

"Thanks, Duncan, that was very generous of you. In return, I'd like to show you how to fight with a knife."

"Sure. Go right ahead."

Paaaina then demonstrated knife techniques, as well we how to disarm and fight a knife-wielding opponent.

"David, this is very good. It is a typical military approach with the opponent charging in. But to fight someone who really knows how to handle a knife, someone expert in knife fighting, it doesn't work. The way you fight with a knife, you have no chance against me."

"What?" He was shocked, unable to believe it.

"The only way is to show you," Duncan offered.

Paaaina was amazed at Duncan's agility with a knife, and even more startled at how easily he – a SEAL instructor teaching hand-to-hand combat – was disarmed and subdued.

Paaaina was so impressed he went to the top brass. Several weeks later, Duncan was invited to teach knife-fighting techniques to Navy SEAL Teams Two and Four. He was to teach them many years thereafter. Most of the techniques he taught, incidentally, were not *Wing Chun*. They were the killing techniques he had learned from the mysterious old man.

David K. Paaaina is now retired, and to this day remains Duncan's good friend.

Chapter 34

SWAT Come Along

Norfolk
1977

Learning without thinking is superfluous
Thinking without learning is perilous
學 而 不 思 則 罔　思 而 不 學 則 殆
(*xue er bu si ze wang; si er bu xue ze dai*)
The Analects of Confucius
Confucius

When Confucius said: "Learning without thinking is superfluous; thinking without learning is perilous", he did not have *Kung Fu* in mind.

Over the years, many theories which people took for granted have been proven invalid by those who bothered to think, question and test. One can imagine the disastrous consequences of an unworkable military strategy in battle or an untested fighting technique in combat. It is suicidal. It is dangerous to accept a combat technique without first proving it works.

As far as *Kung Fu* is concerned, perhaps it would be more appropriate to say "Learning without thinking is *perilous,* thinking without learning is *superfluous.*"

The following is a good example.

Police chiefs from around the nation were present at an FBI barbecue to which Duncan had been invited. Someone corralled Duncan for a demonstration: "Let Duncan show us something." He requested a volunteer and Chief Collier, head of Virginia's Port Authority, stepped forward. Duly impressed with Duncan's demonstration, Collier subsequently arranged for him to instruct the Port Authority Police.

Every two years, the Commonwealth of Virginia hosts an in-service unarmed combat training for the state's police officers. It's an opportunity for sergeants, inspectors, lieutenants and captains from all over Virginia to reacquaint themselves with old techniques and learn new ones. Attendance is mandatory for State Police instructors. In 1977, since he was teaching the Port Authority police at the Regional Police Academy in Norfolk, Duncan attended.

The seminar leader was an African-American officer with an excellent reputation for his knowledge of unarmed combat. Built like a linebacker, he delivered a good speech, afterwards demonstrating various techniques, and concluded by inviting questions from his audience.

There were no questions. Apparently everyone had it down cold. Perhaps catching his attention as the only Chinese there, the seminar leader asked Duncan what he thought of the technique known as *Come Along*. He was, no doubt, expecting a stock answer – 'Great' or 'Very effective' – instead of Duncan's "It doesn't work."

"What do you mean? This technique has been in service longer than you!" He sounded annoyed, and the rest of the audience was not impressed with the comment either.

"Why don't you try it on me and see if it works?" Duncan offered.

Come Along is a simple technique used to subdue a suspect

by flexing his wrist inward so that his hand becomes inverted downward. By putting the subdued forearm between your forearm and your flank while keeping the hand inverted with your other hand, pressure is put on the nerve, inviting acquiescence. The two of you walk in a fashion as if you were holding hands. In reality, suspects are all handcuffed.

Duncan arose, went to the front of the room, and the instructor attempted to impose *Come Along*. It failed. He was unable to invert Duncan's hand at the wrist, no matter how hard he tried. The instructor was both surprised and perplexed. So were the other officers. Now they seemed to be paying attention.

"You are right. It doesn't work," he agreed somewhat dejectedly.

"You are wrong. Of course it works," replied Duncan.

"What are you talking about?" Now he was really confused.

"Only if you know how to do it right."

Somewhat testily, the instructor asked: "What do you mean 'do it right'?"

"It is simple. When you gentlemen practice on each other, you cooperate. You offer no resistance, but that's not realistic. The suspects don't necessarily cooperate."

There was total silence. They were waiting for Duncan to let them in on the secret.

Breaking the stillness, the instructor asked: "How should we do it?"

"Make them cooperate," Duncan blithely responded.

"But how?"

He proceeded to show them how. He grabbed the leader's right wrist with his left hand, attempting to invert it. The leader naturally resisted with all his might. Duncan suddenly feinted a choke to his throat with the other hand, causing him to reflexively jerk his head backward, dissipating any resistance at the wrist. The diversion succeeded and *Come Along* worked smoothly. The key, of course, was to divert the suspect's attention with the implied greater threat.

Duncan was treated to a genuine round of applause.

Leung diverted the instructor's attention by feinting a choke to his throat

The instructor jerked his head back...

...dissipating any resistance at the wrist

Come Along succeeded

Chapter 35

Endgame

Hong Kong
2002

An old *thousand-li* horse crouching in the stable
Aspires to gallop a thousand *li*
老 驥 伏 櫪 志 在 千 里
(*lao ji fu li zhi zai qi li*)
Cao Cao (曹操, 155-220)

Cao Cao, a controversial figure in the Three Kingdoms Period (220-265), became the King of Wei. He was one of the legendary figures in Chinese history who were adept in both pen and sword (文武全才 *wen wu quan cai*); well versed in both literary and military skills. In the verses quoted above, Cao Cao evokes the image of an old but vigorous *thousand-li* horse not yet ready to be put out to pasture. Though getting old, he still nurtures high aspirations.

At the age of 60, Duncan Leung could look back on a turbulent but satisfying martial arts career. He had long since exhausted his appetite for challenges in combat. There was nothing left to prove in this regard. He had come to the rescue of the innocent and weak when the situation demanded it. He had traveled to almost every continent, training civilians and members of government agencies including SWAT teams, U.S. Navy SEALs, police officers, FBI agents, and elite army units; his *Wing Chun* descendants numbered in the thousands. At this stage in life, Duncan looked forward to spending more time with his family, concentrating on his commercial activities, and winding down his hitherto grueling teaching schedule.

Not prone to nostalgia, Duncan was philosophical about the turning of the wheel. A forward-looking individual, he understood that times change and social conditions do not remain static. As the older generation inevitably died out, he observed the waning of the art of *Wing Chun*, even as he considered himself a holdover from an era that was fast disappearing.

But destiny, which had so often played a decisive role in his life, was not yet ready to release its grip on Duncan Leung. Perhaps there was a karmic obligation on his part to repay the good fortune which had consistently blessed his martial arts career.

In recent years, *San Da* championships have become popular events in China. China lobbied for *San Da* to become an Olympic event in the year 2008, when China would host the Olympic Games in Beijing.

San Da is a form of Free Fight. It looks similar to Thai boxing. Participants wear gloves and shorts, but fight barefooted. They are allowed to fight with their fists, feet and knees. But unlike Thai boxers, they are not permitted to use their elbows. *San Da* fighters may grab their opponents like wrestlers and flip them over to score points.

Promoters have successfully aroused public interest in *San Da* tournaments, particularly on television, similar to wrestling in the west. From a commercial point of view it is unquestionably a success. However, as a promotion of *Kung Fu*, it is a total disaster. Chinese boxers look awesome when competing among themselves, but are easily disposed of in international Free Fight championships. What Chinese viewers cannot understand is why the Chinese fighters' *Kung Fu* doesn't even look like Chinese martial arts. Their fighting style is a mixture of Thai boxing, *Tae Kwon Do*, wrestling and some *Kung Fu*. Adopting other martial arts at the expense of *Kung Fu* is the core problem. No wonder Chinese fighters and their fighting styles are considered ineffective and weak.

The Chinese government is responsible for the present pitiful state of Chinese martial arts, because since October 1949 Chinese citizens have been prohibited from practicing *Kung Fu* for combat purposes. China produces many *Performing Kung Fu* instructors whose unproven fighting techniques are becoming increasingly more difficult to perform, though spectacular to watch. However, they are not qualified to teach combat when they themselves have no genuine combat experience, and the effectiveness of their fighting techniques remain untested.

It broke Duncan's heart to watch Chinese combatants being regularly demolished by other martial arts practitioners, especially Thai boxers, considering China's history as the birthplace of the great martial arts traditions. They could not apply their fighting techniques effectively in the ring. Worse still, Chinese combatants were looking and fighting more like Thai boxers and wrestlers. There were hardly any discernible traces of *Kung Fu* in their fighting arsenal. Without an *Applied Kung Fu* Bo Le, every Chinese *thousand-li* horse's talents will go undeveloped because he is learning unproven techniques.

In 2001, Duncan Leung decided for the first time to discuss his life in martial arts and fighting episodes in order to reveal the existence of *Applied Wing Chun*. He determined to discover *thousand-li* horses so that he could pass on his knowledge to future generations and prove to the world that *Kung Fu* can be effective and applicable in Free Fight tournaments.

In the third year of the third millennium – 2002 – Duncan accepted an unenviable task. He agreed to teach six Chinese youngsters *Applied Wing Chun* and train them to become fighters capable of winning *San Da* and Free Fight tournaments within a period of two years. Thus, on the verge of withdrawing from martial arts in his seventh decade, Duncan undertook a new challenge.

Stephen Falkner, a formal disciple of Duncan, was the ideal person to assist his *Sifu* in accomplishing what most people would consider an impossible mission. A third-generation German-American, Steve began to study *Applied Wing Chun* under Duncan at the age of 19, soon after his father passed away. Over the next 20 years he amassed ample fighting experience and became known for his thoroughness and patience in teaching.

Steve was honored and excited when he was called upon to participate in this noble cause. Without hesitation he quit his job in Florida, packed his bags and traveled thousands of miles with his newly-wed physiotherapist wife Nancy to live in a relatively primitive village in southern China. Steve began supervising the teaching and training of six non-English speaking teenagers for little remuneration. While feeling terrible guilt over leaving his beloved mother alone in a Florida nursing home, his sacrifice and total commitment did not go unnoticed.

Duncan and Steve did this not for fame or fortune; only to set an example so that Chinese martial arts' *hidden dragons and crouching tigers* may volunteer to come forward, offering themselves to teach their applicable *Kung Fu* to future generations to help the revival of Chinese martial arts.

Mission Impossible

Foshan
2008

Success and failure caused by the same factor
成 也 蕭 何 敗 也 蕭 何
(*cheng ye Xiao He, bai ye Xiao He*)

Xiao He (蕭何), the first prime minister of the Han Dynasty (206 B.C. - 220 A.D.), was instrumental in recommending the great general Han Xin (韓信) to the first emperor of the dynasty, as well as in orchestrating Han Xin's death. This gave birth to this proverb, used when the success and failure of a person is caused by the same factor.

When *Wing Chun Warrior* was first published in 2003, I was hoping that one day a publisher would be interested enough to ask me to write the sequel to the *Endgame*. Five years later, Blacksmith Books gave me the opportunity to close the final chapter.

Han Yu (see Chapter 10) said "Only when there is a Bo Le can there be a *thousand-li* horse. While *thousand-li* horses are not common, men like Bo Le are even rarer."

When Han Yu made this statement, he was a frustrated minister, having been banished by his emperor to govern a remote county 8,000 *li* from the capital. As an accomplished scholar, Han Yu had always prided himself as a man of ability, a *thousand-li* horse, meant to serve his king and country at the center of power. Unfortunately, the emperor he served did not have the foresight of Bo Le.

The following is a story of a successful modern-day Bo Le and his *thousand-li* horse:

Liu Xiang is a born athlete. His talents were recognized long before he won the all-round national junior championships in track and field in 1998 at the age of 15. The question was in which event he should specialize. Liu was handpicked by the national coach and sports committee to specialize in the high jump, an event in which Zhu Jianhua had won bronze at the Los Angeles Olympics in 1984. From then on, Liu trained hard, preparing himself for the Athens Olympic high jump event in 2004 with little prospect of winning. But *yuan* – destiny – intervened in 1999.

Sun Haiping, the 110-meter hurdle coach, had been watching Liu in training. It was obvious to him that Liu was in the wrong hand for the wrong event. Somehow, Sun was able to spot the hurdler in Liu and could see Liu's potential was ready to explode. With courage and conviction, Sun succeeded in persuading Liu, Liu's parents, Liu's coach and the sports committee to let him take over and coach Liu for the 110-meter hurdles – an event no Chinese athlete had even come close to winning! As a matter of fact, no Chinese male athlete had ever won an Olympic gold medal in track and field before the Athens Games.

Sun proved that he is a modern-day Bo Le by discovering and grooming his *thousand-li* horse to victory. Liu Xiang won gold and broke the Olympic and world record in Athens. He became a national hero for winning China's first track and field Olympic gold medal.

With regard to Duncan Leung's ambition of coaching six youngsters to become world-class combatants within a period of two years, we have to give him credit for attempting the impossible with sheer courage and conviction, not to mention the time factor. Unfortunately, courage and conviction alone were not enough to create champions. Two essential elements – a Bo Le and a *thousand-li* horse – were required, but they were both missing in his squad. Without these vital elements, the mission was doomed to failure before it began.

To make matters worse, the six high-school dropouts in his charge were afraid of pain and scared to fight, and they found endurance training a real hardship. The fact that they were soundly defeated after two years of training by *San Da* competitors at the youth level did not surprise anyone.

The champion combatant is not created out of the ordinary. Mike Tyson, for example, was a prodigy. His potential was obvious to the legendary trainer Cus D'Amato. It still took D'Amato five years to create the perfect heavyweight fighter. D'Amato's death in 1985 did not change Tyson's destiny: he became the youngest heavyweight champion ever when he gained the World Boxing Council championship a year later.

It is safe to conclude that there is no invincible fighting technique, only ageless ideals – as we see in Bruce Lee, whose admirable contribution to martial arts continues to bring happiness and excitement to millions all over the world, even so many years after his passing.

About the Author

Ken Ing, M.D., is a medical doctor who graduated from the University of London in 1970, practised in Canada and Hong Kong, and retired in 1997. He was introduced to Duncan Leung in 1999, unaware that he was meeting a master of *Wing Chun Kung Fu*. It was only a couple of years later that the author discovered Duncan's real background, at which point his dream of assisting in the transmission of this martial art to future generations was born.